Reimagining
Collaboration

Reimagining Collaboration

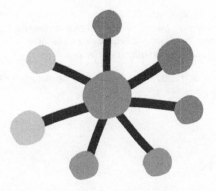

Slack, Microsoft Teams, Zoom, and the Post-COVID World of Work

Phil Simon

**Award-winning author of *The Age of the Platform*
and *Message Not Received***

Reimagining Collaboration: Slack, Microsoft Teams, Zoom, and the Post-COVID World of Work

For information about this title or to order other books and/or electronic media, contact the publisher:

MOTION

Motion Publishing | www.motionpub.com

ISBNs:
978-0-9829302-8-1 (hardcover)
978-0-9829302-2-9 (paperback)
978-0-9829302-7-4 (eBook)

Printed in the United States of America

Cover design: Luke Fletcher | www.fletcherdesigns.com
Interior design: 1106 Design

Also by Phil Simon

ZOOM FOR DUMMIES

SLACK FOR DUMMIES

ANALYTICS:
The Agile Way

MESSAGE NOT RECEIVED:
Why Business Communication Is Broken and How to Fix It

THE VISUAL ORGANIZATION:
Data Visualization, Big Data, and the Quest
for Better Decisions

TOO BIG TO IGNORE:
The Business Case for Big Data

THE AGE OF THE PLATFORM:
How Amazon, Apple, Facebook, and Google
Have Redefined Business

THE NEW SMALL:
How a New Breed of Small Businesses Is Harnessing
the Power of Emerging Technologies

THE NEXT WAVE OF TECHNOLOGIES:
Opportunities in Chaos

WHY NEW SYSTEMS FAIL:
An Insider's Guide to Successful IT Projects

Praise for

Reimagining Collaboration

"An insightful perspective on the new world of work. Collaboration is more essential than ever, and Phil Simon provides the roadmap we need."

—**DORIE CLARK**, author of *Entrepreneurial You* and executive
education faculty, Duke University Fuqua School of Business

"Phil Simon's latest book not only defines collaboration with a depth and breadth never before seen, it defines the future of work in tomorrow's successful organizations. *Reimagining Collaboration* is a must-read not only for those leading knowledge management and productivity efforts, but for every business leader in any organization."

—**DOUG LANEY**, Innovation Fellow, West Monroe Partners
and author of *Infonomics: How to Monetize, Manage, and
Measure Information as an Asset for Competitive Advantage*

"You will love *Reimagining Collaboration, a* humor-filled yet perceptive journey into the remarkably collaborative future of work. Simon's framework and practical tips will help your team move from good to better to best."

—**DR. MARY DONOHUE**, founder of The Digital Wellness Center
and author of *Message Received: 7 Steps to Break Down
Communication*

"At one time or another, I've used many of the tools discussed in this book. I just didn't fully appreciate the bigger picture. *Reimagining Collaboration* made me appreciate the true power of these collaborative technologies—especially when used together."

—**BRIAN SOMMER**, technology industry analyst and author of
Digital With Impact

"Solutionists believe that new technologies magically solve major challenges by themselves. Of course, they're wrong. Effective collaboration is a nuanced, multidimensional problem—a point that Phil Simon makes in spades. Ultimately, *Reimagining Collaboration* delivers on its promise: To make readers not only think differently about this essential subject, but provide a framework for actually doing it."

—**MIKE VARDY**, founder of Productivityist and author of *The Gift of Time*

"The perfect handbook for anyone who has to work with teammates on a job or project."

—**THE BOOKLIFE PRIZE**

"Using tools like Zoom, Slack, and Trello doesn't mean you are "collaborating" well. This excellent read will challenge you to stop relying upon email and actually connect the tools that allow us to work together in meaningful way."

—**KARIN M. REED**, author *Suddenly Virtual: Making Remote Meetings Work* and CEO of Speaker Dynamics

"Simon's Hub-Spoke Model of Collaboration will change the way you think about internal communications and productivity forever."

—**JOHN JANTSCH**, author of *Duct Tape Marketing*

To the frontline workers battling COVID-19.
You are true heroes.

"Never attribute to malice that which can be adequately explained by ignorance."

—HANLON'S RAZOR

Contents

Introduction   xix

Part I: *The Collaboration Imperative*   1

Chapter 1: The Evolution of Collaboration   3

Chapter 2: Collaboration in Context   19

Chapter 3: The Benefits of Reimagining Collaboration   43

Chapter 4: Why Email Inhibits Collaboration   51

Part II: *Better Collaboration Through
Technology*   61

Chapter 5: Reimagining Workplace Technology   63

Chapter 6: The Hub-Spoke Model of Collaboration   79

Chapter 7: How to Select an Internal Collaboration Hub 99

Chapter 8: Why Collaboration Hubs Can Disappoint   117

Part III: *Moving From Theory to Practice*   127

Chapter 9: Reviewing Implementation Strategies   129

Chapter 10: Reimagining Business Processes   139

Chapter 11: Collaboration Killers and How to Handle Them   153

Chapter 12: The Myths of Collaboration   167

Chapter 13: Reimagining Communication and Human
Resources   183

Part IV: *What Now?*   195

Chapter 14: Why Effective Collaboration Requires Lifelong
Learning   197

Chapter 15: The Future of Collaboration   207

Chapter 16: Recommendations for Reimagining
Collaboration   221

Conclusion and Parting Words   229

Thank-You   231

Suggested Reading   233

Acknowledgments   235

About the Author   237

Index   239

Endnotes   249

List of Figures and Tables

Figure 1.1:   Percentage of Americans Working Remotely   10

Figure 1.2:   U.S. Cities With Biggest Percentage Gains in
Net Arrivals   13

Figure 1.3:   U.S. Cities With Steepest Percentage Declines
in Net Arrivals   13

Figure 2.1:   The Dimensions of Collaboration   36

Figure 5.1:   Zoom's Insane User Growth   67

Figure 5.2:   Aging in Reverse   75

Figure 6.1:   The Hub-Spoke Model of Collaboration   85

Figure 6.2:   Zoom Zapps   85

Figure 6.3:   Power Automate Template to Post Email to
Microsoft Teams   89

Figure 7.1:   Collaboration Hubs and Diminishing Marginal
Returns   105

Table 7.1:   The Three Fields of Enterprise Technology
Adoption   112

Figure 12.1: My YouCanBook.me Page   173

Figure 15.1: Microsoft Teams' Together Mode   216

Figure 15.2: Breakdown of Employee Work Preferences   219

Table 16.1:   Collaboration Maturity Model   222

Figure 16.1: Tools Matter   223

Figure 16.2: Size (Probably) Matters   224

Internal collaboration hub (n):

General-use software application designed to promote effective communication and collaboration. Ideally, all organizational conversations, decisions, documents, and institutional knowledge exist in a hub. Critically, hubs connect to different spokes. They enable automation with little-to-no technical skill required. Examples of today's popular hubs include Slack, Microsoft Teams, and Zoom.

Spoke (n):

Software application designed for a specific purpose. Examples include productivity, content creation, customer-relationship management, and project management. Spokes can easily exchange information with hubs, provide status updates, and more. As a result, employee, group, and organization communication and collaboration markedly improve.

Introduction

"You can write a 200-page book about Zoom?"

My friend Tess incredulously asked me this question after I told her that I'd signed a contract to pen *Zoom For Dummies* in April of 2020. (In fact, the book ultimately came in at twice that length because, as I came to learn, Zoom is so much more than a user-friendly videoconferencing application.)

To be fair, Tess's skepticism wasn't entirely unfounded.

As I would soon learn, she was no outlier. Many people didn't—and still don't—fully appreciate the true power of today's collaboration tools—and not just Zoom. My previous book, the equally hefty *Slack For Dummies*, had evoked similar reactions. Some long-time Slack and Zoom users posted online reviews, noting that my book taught them a great deal about what those technologies could do. Even some employees at each company echoed that sentiment.

I have spent the last quarter-century at the nexus of management, collaboration, technology, and data. As a result, I have learned a thing or six about each. For the purposes of this book, people generally use workplace collaboration and communication tech in limited capacities. New applications arrive, but they tend not to alter our habits, and certainly not immediately. And I'm hardly the only person to observe as much.

Meet Eugene Fubini

Eugene Fubini (1913–1997) immigrated from Italy to the United States in 1939. During his career, he helped create U.S. policy during the Cold War. He is perhaps most famous for codifying four principles. *Fubini's Law* states that:

1. People initially use technology to do what they do now—but faster.
2. Then they *gradually* begin to use technology to do new things.
3. The new technology changes how we live and how we work.
4. These changes to how we live and work ultimately change society—and eventually change technology.

The operative word here is *gradually*. As a general rule, when it comes to workplace technology, people of a certain age tend to fight change as long as possible. It takes a black swan for them to fundamentally change how they work.

COVID-19 was such an event.

The Struggle (to Adapt) Is Real

Go back to March of 2020. Think about how you and your colleagues responded when your employer suddenly shut its doors. Did that transition go off without a hitch? If so, then, congratulations are in order. You're one of a relative few.

The struggle to adapt to the new normal was real. It still is. I saw firsthand how woefully unprepared even a purportedly innovative institution was for such a dramatic shift in how its employees work and collaborate.

By way of background, during that surreal period, I was finishing my fourth year as a full-time college professor at Arizona State University's W. P. Carey School of Business. My home base was the Information Systems (IS) Department.

Three facts about COVID-19 and ASU will provide the requisite context. First, oodles of international students attend the school. In 2017, that number approached 14,000, more than any other public university.[1] At any point and depending on geopolitical winds, roughly one in five ASU students calls a country other than the U.S. home.[2] For a long time, ASU and other state universities have heavily recruited foreign students for obvious reasons: These students typically pay fees two to three times higher than their in-state counterparts.[3] Chinese students are particularly prevalent in Arizona.

Second, for the last six years, *U.S. News & World Report* has named ASU the most innovative school in America.[4] Its powers-that-be have never been shy about sharing that accolade with the world. On the contrary, that tagline prominently adorns its website[5] as well as many local buses and billboards. In one example of how it touts its innovation, the school proudly announced that it had procured an enterprise license for the popular collaboration tool Slack in January 2019—well before a single documented coronavirus case anywhere in the world.

Third, media outlets such as *The New York Times* reported dozens of coronavirus cases in China as early as June of 2019.[6]

Brass tacks: COVID-19 was coming to American universities including ASU. It was a matter of *when*, not *if*.

Let's take a step back and summarize:

1. The most innovative university in the country sports a large international contingent.
2. Many of these students are Chinese and had returned from their homeland in January of 2020, after the winter break.
3. ASU had recently purchased a powerful new collaboration tool.
4. University leadership conservatively had more than three months to war-game the inevitable arrival of COVID-19.

Against this backdrop, surely ASU could shift all of its courses online with minimal disruption to faculty and students alike, right?

From the outside looking in, you might think so.

And you would be spectacularly wrong.

When ASU announced the indefinite suspension of in-person classes in the middle of spring break of 2020, utter chaos ensued. It took only a few days for orderly processes, normal activities, and established deadlines to devolve into widespread confusion. Specifically, and in no particular order:

- ● The administration's hastily arranged Zoom and Slack training classes didn't staunch the bleeding. Many professors skipped them because they had other fish to fry. No surprise here. It's impossible to fix the plane while it's in the air. Overall class quality and student learning plummeted.*
- ● Department-wide webinars left faculty members with more questions than answers.
- ● ASU discouraged thousands of students from returning to their dorms. Some of them could not even retrieve their textbooks.
- ● One student filed a class-action lawsuit claiming breach of contract and demanding tuition and housing refunds.[7]
- ● Administrators' guidance to faculty was anything but clear. As but one example, some professors subsequently offered their students pass/fail options. Others refused.
- ● Students clamored for exceptions, extensions, and do-overs—some legitimate, others because coronavirus ate their homework.

Lest I paint an overly negative picture of my former employer, a few disclaimers are in order. First, every institution of higher learning struggled in the immediate wake of COVID-19. It's not like there was a playbook to follow. They weren't opening a local Subway or Arby's. School presidents were making things up on the fly.

---

* Department chairs broke precedent and intentionally ignored student evaluations when making decisions to extend offers to existing non-tenured faculty.

Second, let's say that every ASU professor had been proficient in Slack and Zoom. Managing the situation still would have been challenging, given the school's massive student population: 90,000 in-person and 38,000 online at the end of 2019.[8]

The Bill for Years of Inertia Finally Comes Due

Since the fall of 2017, I had used Slack in all of my classes.* I had encouraged my colleagues to use it as well, admittedly without much success. During my tenure at ASU, only a handful of my IS colleagues had warmed to it. I suspect that professors in the Philosophy and English departments sported even lower adoption rates.

> *"We shape our tools, and, thereafter, they shape us."*
> —MARSHALL McLUHAN

Although disappointing, at least the party line was consistent. A few times since I had started, I asked department decision-makers why we relied exclusively on '90s-style email and attachments for internal communications, especially after ASU had purchased a far better tool. After all, we were the IS department, damn it. Shouldn't we be setting an example for the rest of the university by embracing Slack?

They hemmed and hawed. Fundamentally, they didn't want to learn new programs and change their antiquated business

---

* Read my post on the topic at https://bit.ly/hsc-slack.

processes, conditions that I had diagnosed many times in my consulting career. Professors and staff kept using their email for internal communication and "collaboration."

McLuhan was right.

The Revelation

Fast-forward to mid-April of 2020. As finals approached, all things considered, my semester was progressing fairly smoothly, especially in comparison to those of my colleagues. In part, I could thank my proficiency with Slack and my decision to continue using it at the beginning of the semester. I didn't have to introduce my students to a new communication tool in the midst of the chaos. (Also, in the interest of full disclosure, the department had assigned me four online classes that semester. I had already recorded my requisite videos in January, well before the shit hit the fan.)

Outside of the classroom, I was knee-deep in researching and writing *Zoom For Dummies*. At that point, I used Slack, Zoom, and Microsoft Teams daily in different capacities—the three most popular collaboration hubs in the world.

I had noticed how the three applications were far more similar than dissimilar. Indeed, they shared much of the same core functionality. It occurred to me that the specific tools that organizations, groups, and individuals use to collaborate certainly matter, just not as much as most people think. (The only caveat: As long as they don't attempt to "collaborate" via email, but we'll tackle that topic in Chapter 4.)

Focusing on the features of a specific application certainly made sense when writing a *For Dummies* book. In a way, though, that approach obscured a more important reality: As I witnessed firsthand at ASU, fusing new tools with antiquated habits and business processes didn't magically make groups, departments, or entire organizations more collaborative. By themselves, applications don't rewire our tried-and-true habits.

Let me draw a golf parallel. Say that your swing is horrendous. When you take the club back, you don't know where the ball will ultimately land. Buying a pricey new driver won't make you any less of a hack. You might even hit the ball *farther* out of bounds. Rather, to become proficient or even competent at the sport, you'll have to break your bad habits and learn new techniques.

At that point, the big idea at the center of this book began taking shape. Compared to my last two, I envisioned a shorter, tool-agnostic text that would offer manifold benefits.

What You Should Know From the Get-Go

I believe in truth in advertising. To this end, know this: *Reimagining Collaboration* provokes and challenges its readers. It intentionally questions conventional and deep-rooted assumptions about how we communicate and collaborate at work, such as:

- All text-based communication is essentially the same, irrespective of the application used.
- The tools that people use to communicate and collaborate are inherently personal and don't affect others in the organization.

- Asynchronous communication and collaboration are just as effective as their synchronous counterparts.
- It's technically demanding and time-consuming to stitch together different applications.

Chapter 12 explores these myths in far more depth.

I want you to look at communicating and collaborating through a very different lens. If you do, then you'll reevaluate a number of things. First up is your existing relationship with workplace technology. Why do you keep switching back and forth among different applications? Why aren't all of your tools connected—or at least most of them?

Beyond that, in all likelihood, you'll never view your existing business processes in the same way. I suspect that you'll want to redesign many of them.

In short, this book asks if we can do better.

Reimagining Collaboration is conceptual in nature. In this way, it represents a vast departure from my recent forays into the *For Dummies* world. Because of the rapid pace of software updates today, my last two books are on burning planks. This one, however, should hold up for the foreseeable future, regardless of vendors' changes to their user interfaces.

In a similar vein, this book is technology agnostic by design. The following pages are equally relevant for employees who work in Microsoft, Google, Slack, or Zoom shops—or even if their companies have not deployed one as of now. If you're looking for tips on how to use those internal collaboration hubs, you won't find them here.

xxviii   Reimagining Collaboration

Who Should Read This Book?

In no particular order, I wrote *Reimagining Collaboration* with these audiences in mind:

- Your team, department, or employer sucks at collaboration and internal communication. You're searching for a better way to work with your colleagues and partners.
- You mistakenly believe that effective collaboration entails hitting "Reply All" on an email thread.
- Your organization has deployed Microsoft Teams, Slack, Zoom, or another internal collaboration hub. Six months later, however, collaboration is still wanting.
- Your organization or team is thinking of deploying one of these hubs.
- You have adopted new, collaborative technologies and processes at work. You want your colleagues to do the same.

If you fall into one of these groups, then *Reimagining Collaboration* is right up your alley. I don't guarantee results, but you will look at collaboration through a new lens.

What Will You Learn?

This book does not lack ambition. *Reimagining Collaboration* introduces a fundamentally different model for workplace collaboration and communication. You'll learn how to think about these subjects, as well as technology and business processes, in a holistic way. I don't just introduce a new model, though. You'll learn how to put it into action—and how to handle people who are stuck in their ways.

Plan of Attack

Part I of this book ("The Collaboration Imperative") provides an insanely brief history of collaboration, technology, and the workplace. It contrasts collaboration with adjacent work-related terms. I make the case that collaboration today matters more than ever. Only by eschewing email can we realize the benefits of true collaboration.

In Part II ("Better Collaboration Through Technology"), I explain how new breed of tools that I dub *internal collaboration hubs*—hence, this book's subtitle—makes it far easier for employees to work together. The big three are Slack, Microsoft Teams, and Zoom.

I also introduce the fulcrum at the center of this book: the Hub-Spoke Model of Collaboration. You'll learn how to easily stitch different applications together without any coding. By doing so, you'll minimize rework, automate tasks, and quickly get on the same page as your colleagues. Oh, and you'll communicate and collaborate much better, too.

At its core, *Reimagining Collaboration* is disruptive. It forces its readers to think differently about work. It advocates adopting new habits and technologies. In that vein, Part III ("Moving From Theory to Practice") explains its major consequences: Organizations will have to rethink legacy business processes and confront problematic and change-averse employees. I also offer suggestions about how to maximize the chance that the new collaboration hub will take root.

As you'll learn in the following pages, neither collaboration hubs nor their spokes are static. They evolve in interesting ways. To this end, Part IV ("What Now?") puts a bow on the book. I offer advice on how to quickly learn new tools—and new features of existing applications. I also chime in with some predictions on the future of collaboration technologies. The internal collaboration hubs will become only smarter, more connected, and more powerful. I end with some tips designed to improve collaboration and a call to action.

I hope that you enjoy *Reimagining Collaboration* and learn a great deal from it.

Part I

The Collaboration Imperative

Chapter

The Evolution of Collaboration

*"The future is already here—it's just
not evenly distributed."*

—WILLIAM GIBSON

Long before we stood upright, collaboration was essential to our species' survival. Since the dawn of our existence, we have worked together in some capacity.

How do I know?

Simple. Because I wouldn't be here without collaboration. Neither would you or anyone else for that matter. But don't take my word for it.

Cavemen and Collaboration

Archaeologists know that, two million years ago, members of *Homo erectus* needed to work together in order to survive. Put differently, collaboration wasn't optional. Hunter-gatherers' challenges included foraging for food and water, finding shelter, keeping warm, and staving off wild animals. Hunters gotta hunt, right?

Around 10,000 years ago, our ancestors developed a new and better means of providing subsistence: farming. At a high level, the Agricultural Revolution required *Homo sapiens* to work together. As Yuval Noah Harari writes in his bestselling book *Sapiens: A Brief History of Humankind*:

> Wheat didn't like rocks and pebbles, so *Sapiens* broke their backs clearing fields. Wheat didn't like sharing its space, water, and nutrients with other plants, so men and women labored long days weeding under the scorching sun.

Of course, today relatively few of us call ourselves *farmers*. As of this writing, they represent a mere 1.3 percent of the U.S. workforce.[1] No matter. As Harari describes, collaboration wasn't easy millions of years ago, but we did it because it was essential. Notably, we also worked together *in person* because, again, what other option was there? Cavemen didn't whip out their smartphones, fire up Google Docs, or text each other.

Early Office-Based Collaboration

Fast-forward 10 millennia or so to about 1950. People were much more likely to work in offices than in the fields. Picture *Mad Men*. Like agrarians, though, most professionals worked in close physical proximity to their colleagues.

During this quaint era, people could certainly exchange information and ideas. That is, they could collaborate *synchronously.* Doing so, however, meant that they needed to meet in an office, board trains or planes, or pick up the phone.

As for *asynchronous* work, typewriters and intra- and inter-office memos ruled the day. Friction abounded. Executives typically employed secretaries to make appointments, coordinate schedules, and handle other administrative work. Mainframe computers existed, but they were enormously expensive, rare, bulky, and limited by 1990s standards, let alone those of today.

New Technologies and Tools Change the Game

This model of decidedly low-tech collaboration began to shift around 1995. Although early incarnations of the Internet had existed since the mid-1960s, it was largely the purview of academics and government types.

A few things happened that brought the Internet and high-speed communications to the consumer and business worlds. Most notably Sir Tim Berners-Lee invented the World Wide Web in 1989. Marc Andreessen and Eric Bina launched Mosaic, the insanely popular and user-friendly web browser, in February of 1993.

To be sure, the Internet and the Web changed many things.[*] Photo-development services, travel agents, fax machines, most bank tellers, executive secretaries, and Blockbuster Videos largely went the way of the Dodo. Within a relatively

---

[*] Don't conflate the two. The Web is the software that sits upon the hardware that is the Internet.

short period of time, laptops, e-commerce sites, sophisticated productivity software, nascent videoconferencing tools, search engines, social networks, blogs, smartphones, tablets, email, websites, and file-sharing services arrived.

For the purposes of this book, these powerful new tools meant that synchronous workplace collaboration no longer needed to occur in person. For its part, asynchronous collaboration became quicker and easier. In a word, collaboration was becoming more *virtual*.

The Turn of the Century Births Purely Distributed Companies

Plenty of companies and individuals resisted these fundamental changes in how they worked—by themselves and with others. No shocker here.

For example, in 1998, I worked at Merck & Co., one of the largest pharmaceutical companies in the world. I vividly remember Jonas (a pseudonym), a less-than-tech-savvy vice president of human resources. He effectively used his laptop as a paperweight. Jonas told his secretary to print out his emails. He handwrote his responses for her to type.

Back then, such behavior was not exactly the paragon of efficiency. Still, it was understandable and not uncommon.

At the other end of the technology-adoption spectrum, some prescient individuals immediately recognized the vast possibilities that these new tools presented. As a result, they went all-in on tech. These *distributed companies* built collaboration and tech-savviness into their DNA from day one. Here are two of them.

Basecamp

In 1999, Jason Fried, Carlos Segura, and Ernest Kim started 37signals—a web-design firm. Over the years, the company has released a number of different software applications. In February of 2014, it shifted its focus to its project-management tool, Basecamp, and rebranded under that name.

Today, Fried and David Heinemeier Hansson (aka, *DHH*) run the company. DHH currently lives in Benahavís, Spain, while Fried calls Chicago, Illinois, his home. Its other fifty-some employees live wherever they want and rely extensively on collaboration tools.

DHH and Fried have codified their philosophy into a number of bestselling manifestos, most notably *Rework* and *Remote: Office Not Required.* In short, they find the notion that all work needs to take place in the same physical space at the same time absurd.

Automattic

You may not have heard of Matt Mullenweg, but you've doubtless used his company's software. Automattic maintains WordPress—the open-source content-management system that runs a full 39 percent of the world's websites, more than 60 million in total.[2] WordPress provides the plumbing behind *The New York Times*, BBC America, the Rolling Stones, and oodles more household names. On a personal level, I've been using WordPress for a decade. It's awesome.

If you think that Automattic is no five-person startup, trust your instincts. As of May 2020, it employed 1,184 people. One thing, however, hasn't changed: Since its founding in August

2005, Mullenweg has proselytized remote work. Automattic has operated as a purely distributed company from day one.

So, employees never meet each other, right?

Nope.

Each year, everyone descends upon an exotic locale for the company's annual gala. My friend Scott Berkun spent a year working at Automattic on a participative-journalism project. As he writes in his 2013 book *The Year Without Pants: WordPress.com and the Future of Work*:

> The rest of the year we work online from wherever in the world each of us happened to be.[*]

By definition, Automattic employees must collaborate well, or the company would fail. It's as simple as that.

To be sure, most of the *early* distributed companies shared one common characteristic: In one way or another, they were in the technology business.

Why Effective Collaboration Still Remains Elusive

Employee-management tension today is alive and well. You don't need to be a Marxist to observe as much. Over the past few decades, one source of persistent conflict has been remote work. Employees have long wanted it; managers have generally been loath to sanction it.

---

[*] For an informative podcast with Berkun and Mullenweg, see https://bit.ly/nog-pod1.

Our reasons for wanting to work outside of the office vary. At or near the top of the list, however, is increasing commute times. In 2018, the average U.S. employee spent a record 225 hours—*more than nine full days*—traveling to and from work.[3] At the extreme, some supercommuters slogged a mind-boggling two or more hours each way to the office.

With this in mind, you have might expected the majority of employers to have offered flexible work arrangements years ago. I'm talking about relatively minor concessions, such as four-day workweeks and occasionally working from home.

Let's see what the data says.

Not Remotely Prepared for Remote Work

In May of 2019, Harvard Business School and Boston Consulting Group released a lengthy study called "Future Positive: How Companies Can Tap Into Employee Optimism to Navigate Tomorrow's Workplace." The two organizations surveyed 11,000 workers and 6,500 business leaders.[4]

One of the study's findings is particularly apropos here: People consistently voiced their preference for remote work. Sadly, a mere 30 percent of those surveyed indicated that their businesses were prepared to even offer it.

Then COVID-19 happened.

Forced Adoption of New Collaboration Tools

> *"There are decades where nothing happens; and there are weeks in which decades happen."*
> —Vladimir Ilyich Lenin

Hundreds of millions of people across the globe suddenly found themselves in the middle of the greatest work-from-home experiment in history. Here's the data from the United States:

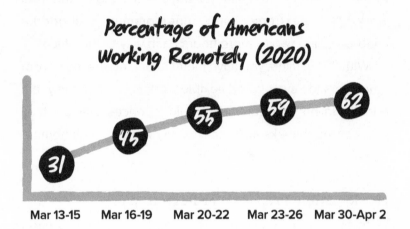

Percentage of Americans
Working Remotely (2020)

31   45   55   59   62

Mar 13-15   Mar 16-19   Mar 20-22   Mar 23-26   Mar 30-Apr 2

Source: *Gallup Panel, 2020.*

FIGURE 1.1: Percentage of Americans Working Remotely

Faced with no other option, organizations reluctantly embraced alternative work arrangements. Many of them purchased and rolled out Slack, Zoom, Microsoft Teams, and the other internal collaboration hubs at the core of this book. They had no choice. Lenin was right.

Management permitting employees to work remotely is one thing; getting them to work and collaborate *effectively* outside of the office is another matter altogether. That is, companies weren't flipping a switch. Foolish is the soul who believes otherwise. Successfully navigating and collaborating in this new environment requires new tools, new norms, and, just as important, a new mindset.

Remote-first or -exclusive companies such as Automattic, Basecamp, and Slack didn't miss a beat when COVID-19 hit. For them, very little changed because each firm had established a strong culture predicated on flexible work and collaboration tools. Their workforces had *already* developed the muscle memory necessary to succeed in this new world.

At the risk of oversimplifying, the vast majority of organizations did not. The typical firm was wholly unprepared for the new normal. Ditto for most employees, many of whom struggled applying old tools to dramatically new situations and learning new collaboration software.

Trust Issues

It's worth nothing that plenty of organizations didn't immediately and unequivocally trust their employees to work remotely. On the contrary, employee-surveillance software became more prevalent. From a *Wall Street Journal* article on April 18, 2020:

> Makers of workplace-monitoring products say they have logged an increase in orders since the coronavirus altered life. Rita Selvaggi, chief executive of employee-monitoring software ActivTrak, says more than 1,000 new companies have signed up to use her company's tool in recent weeks.[5]

I get it. It's easy to see why a manager wants to see her employees' daily productivity scores or reports on which ones violated company security policies. Still, I'd bet my house that plenty of organizations prioritized purchasing software that surveilled their workforces over technology that would allow them to collaborate in a completely new environment.

Remote Work Is Here to Stay

> *"Never waste a good crisis."*
> —WINSTON CHURCHILL

As I write these words, we are still in the midst of a global pandemic—the very definition of a *crisis*. Keep in mind, however, that all crises eventually end. At some point—hopefully, soon—there will be a vaccine, and herd immunity will ensue. Things will go back to normal, right?

In some ways, yes. We'll eventually eat at restaurants, get on planes, attend sporting events and concerts, and congregate in groups without fear and masks. When it comes to work, however, the profound effects of COVID-19 will remain with us forever.

The Work Legacy of COVID-19

Ten years from now, I suspect that we'll look back at COVID-19 as follows: It didn't *change* how we work. Rather, it *accelerated* changes that were already taking place.

COVID-19 accentuated the need for people to collaborate from separate environments and time zones. What's more, as a by-product, it increased the rate at which people adopted truly collaborative technologies. To be sure, the applications of the future will certainly change, but COVID-19 may put the final nail in the coffin of '90s-style email-based "collaboration."

The data is unmistakable: In the immediate wake of COVID-19, people began fleeing pricey cities for more affordable ones.

Source: LinkedIn Economic Graph Research.

FIGURE 1.2: U.S. Cities With Biggest Percentage Gains in Net Arrivals

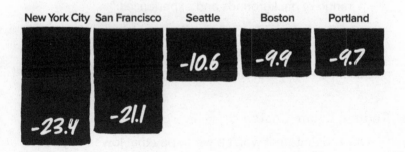

Source: LinkedIn Economic Graph Research.

FIGURE 1.3: U.S. Cities With Steepest Percentage Declines in Net Arrivals

Against this backdrop, companies are increasingly announcing that they will allow their employees to work from home indefinitely. Examples include Adobe, Aetna, Amazon, Facebook, and Zillow.[6] Their management rightfully sees the shift toward remote work not as a problem but as a multi-fold *opportunity*.

Access Larger and More Diverse Talent Pools

First, a truly global workforce allows companies to widen their search for talent. For instance, Facebook no longer needs to compete with Apple, Google, and Twitter for the same limited group of local software engineers and data scientists.

As Pinterest's chief financial officer, Todd Morgenfeld, told *The San Francisco Chronicle* on August 28, 2020:

> As we analyze how our workplace will change in a post-COVID world, we are specifically rethinking where future employees could be based. A more distributed workforce will give us the opportunity to hire people from a wider range of backgrounds and experiences.[7]

A promising candidate in Des Moines, Iowa, might be just as qualified as his brethren in Menlo Park, California.

Reduce Labor Costs

Oh, and Pinterest won't have to pay that Iowan anywhere near the same base salary. As of this writing, the median home price in Des Moines is $140,800.[8] The comparable number in Menlo Park is a cool $2.4 million.[9] Do the math.

In fact, many CXOs are already asking whether their companies need to pay employees their *existing* wages as they relocate to lower-cost areas of the country. On September 11, 2020, Bloomberg QuickTake tweeted the following:

> Twitter, VMware, and other Silicon Valley tech companies are cutting pay for workers leaving the Bay Area for cheaper digs, including an 18% salary decrease for those moving to Denver and an 8% cut for San Diego-bound employees.[10]

Expect this trend to continue—no matter how much people grouse about it.

Lower Corporate Real-Estate Expenditures

Regardless of location, hiring fewer in-person employees lowers corporate real-estate costs. In late August of 2020, Pinterest paid nearly $90 million to terminate a massive 490,000-square-foot lease in a trendy San Francisco district. Expect an increasing number of firms to lease less office space in the future.

Again, the math here is compelling. The general rule of thumb is to allow anywhere between 125 and 225 usable square feet of office space per employee.[11]

Forget New York City, London, San Francisco, and other chic metropolitan areas. Consider downtown Austin, Texas. Paying $50 per square foot per month isn't uncommon. A modest 150-square-foot office costs $7,500 per month. Those expenses drop significantly or disappear altogether if a company embraces remote work.

Position Themselves as Employee-Friendly Places to Work

Lucy is a talented graphic designer and single mother. She's thinking of making a move. Say that two organizations (ABC and XYZ) offer her identical pay, benefits, responsibilities, and room for advancement. ABC insists that Lucy perform all of her work in the office, while XYZ offers considerable flexibility in that regard.

Which job do you think she will take?

Expect many, if not most, organizations to at least partially accommodate their employees' requests for flexible work arrangements. You don't have to be a sorcerer to envision a future with *permanent* hybrid work arrangements. Perhaps Peter will work three days at home and two in the office every week. Michael might work mostly from home and visit the office only for key meetings and brainstorming sessions.

Forced Adoption of Remote Work

In my years as a college professor, Larson Epp distinguished himself as one of my best students. After graduating from ASU in 2017, we remained in touch. Larson didn't move far for his first full-time gig: He accepted a position at his alma mater as a Business Intelligence Analyst.

A year or so into his job, armed with a solid track record, he broached the possibility of working remotely one day per week with his manager, Lou. Unfortunately, Lou had reservations—that is, until COVID-19 forced his hand. At that point, everyone in his department started working from home indefinitely.

Larson proved to Lou that he could be just as productive and collaborative while away from the office. When things return to normal, odds are that Lou will reconsider letting him work remotely.

In a way, nothing has changed from our *Homo sapiens* days: Collaboration is still critical today—whether your primary workplace tool is a tractor, a spatula, or a keyboard.

Chapter Summary

- ●—● When COVID-19 arrived, few companies and their employees were prepared to embrace remote work and, by extension, collaboration.
- ●—● The world of work is not returning to its pre-COVID-19 days. Effective remote work and the tools enabling it will become only *more* prevalent and critical.
- ●—● More remote work increases the importance of reimagining collaboration.

Chapter 2

Collaboration in Context

Collaboration has been with us in some form for millions of years. What's more, the preponderance of work done remotely will abate from its virus-driven acme. If you think that it will disappear altogether, though, think again.

We can't begin to effectively collaborate if we conflate different terms. In order to achieve this goal, it's essential that we fully understand collaboration first.

To this end, this chapter delves into the concept of collaboration, especially in relation to key adjacent terms. It also introduces a simple framework for understanding contemporary collaboration.

Contrasting Collaboration With Adjacent Work-Related Terms

By definition, collaboration doesn't take place in a vacuum. In this way, whether it takes place remotely or in-person is a moot point. What's more, collaboration sits adjacent to a number of other related but distinct terms. A few quick words on each will provide clarity and set the table for the rest of the book.

Communication

At its core, this word means *to make common.*

Let that sink in for a moment.

Now consider the relationship between communication and collaboration. Can you do one without the other?

Yes. Four people can work together on a project without exchanging messages of any kind. Whether communication-free collaboration succeeds, however, is unlikely.

Put differently, communication is a necessary but insufficient condition for successful collaboration. It's just about impossible to collaborate effectively without a decent level of communication. However, good communication does not guarantee successful collaboration.

> ### *The Symbiotic Relationship Between Communication and Collaboration*
>
> In early 2019, a large university in Brazil contacted me via my website about creating a custom data-visualization class to deliver in Porto Alegre during the summer. I was

excited about the opportunity. I hadn't been to Brazil in 20 years.

Over the course of the next few months, my primary contact Luisa and I hashed out the details of my trip and other logistics. I signed a contract and procured a Brazilian visa. Oddly, Luisa sent me two different flight itineraries. I asked which one was valid but never received a straight answer. I kept prodding. In her emails, she wrote that I should stop worrying so much.

A few days before I was scheduled to depart, I still couldn't find my reservation in the airline's website or check in for my flight.

Maybe the language barrier was the problem. (My *español* is pretty solid, but I don't speak Portuguese.) I enlisted the help of my friend Dalton, a Brazilian native. Over Skype, Dalton served as my interpreter and ironed out any miscommunication. Thanks to Dalton's help, I was all set.

Or so I thought.

Fast-forward to departure day. I'm at the Phoenix airport attempting to check in to my flight. I provide Luisa's confirmation number to the attendant at the counter.

Nearly an hour later, several airline employees are trying to find me in their system. The clock is ticking. After finally sorting out that mess, I boarded the plane. I had to repeat the same stressful process in Miami, nearly missing my flight to São Paulo.

Upon finally arriving in Porto Alegre, I met my primary contact Miguel at the luggage carousel. As we talked about the upcoming class, he praised my agenda for day one and asked me what I intended to cover on day two.

Perdão?

In her emails, Luisa had indicated that I would be presenting the same three hours of material on each of the two days; I had not prepared six hours of original content. No matter. All of my students were expecting six, not three. So much for relaxing, adjusting to the different time zone, and taking in the sights. I spent the next 36 hours creating three new hours of material and rehearsing my delivery.

Ultimately, I was able to pull it off. To this day, I receive flattering weekly LinkedIn requests from students who enjoyed my class. It would have gone even better, though, if I hadn't had to scramble at the last minute.

The moral of the story: Effective collaboration is nearly impossible without effective communication.

Cooperation

At a high level and in professional settings, cooperation implies complying with someone else's requests. I'm talking about a passive or decidedly disparate relationship among the organizations, parties, and/or individuals involved.

Let's say that you behaved inappropriately at work. Several employees reported you to HR, and an investigation ensued. In a way, whether you violated company policy is moot. If you fail to cooperate in this scenario, your days are numbered. Suffice it to say that cooperation does not equate to collaboration.

Delegation

You are most certainly familiar with delegation. Your manager gives you a specific task to complete *independently*. By definition, you are not collaborating in this scenario.

Coordination

In some circumstances, someone needs to ensure that several people are all performing a set of tasks in a consistent manner. You've no doubt heard the cliché "Get everyone on the same page."

For example, consider higher education. At large schools, different professors often teach different sections of the same course. It's fairly common for a single course coordinator to meet weekly with the group of professors. Coordinators want each student to learn the same material, irrespective of which faculty member is doing the teaching.

Productivity

You're no doubt familiar with this term. I mean getting things done, completing tasks, and achieving individual goals.

Depending on his role, an employee can be extremely *productive* without being the slightest bit *collaborative*. In fact, some companies pooh-pooh divas precisely because of their unique skills and ability to accomplish key tasks. Netflix, however, is not one of them. As co-founder Reed Hastings has famously said, "We don't tolerate brilliant jerks."

Reclaiming Productivity

When you think about productivity, it wouldn't surprise me if you defined it as a combination of being both effective and efficient. Being productive seems to be all about delivering results consistently, checking off your to-do list at a good pace. Productivity, in essence, is the quality of being productive.

But in our quest to get as much done as possible in as short a time as possible, I believe we've lost sight of the quality aspect of the term. We're focused on quantity first and quality second. When you think about it that way, then productivity is somewhat broken.

How can you truly be productive if the quality of your output is more focused on *how much* than on *how well*? By its very definition, your productivity would be poor.

What if we got back to the core elements of productivity? What if we focused on quality first and quantity second? What would that look like?

I'd suggest it would mean that we'd implement a system to be productive before we implement tools to be productive. So instead of focusing on apps to boost our productivity on their own, we'd bring our system into the apps and let them help us keep that system in line. I suppose you'd say that we'd spend more time focusing on the app within ourselves more than on any other app in our toolkit.

By doing that, we could bring our system to a variety of apps and tools—our own personalized framework—so that we could collaborate with others in ways that involve less friction and more flow. To be sure, you may be required to use a particular app or tool with those you collaborate with—and those tools will vary from collaborator to collaborator. Still, you can figure out how to integrate your system into the tool instead of allowing the tool to initiate an impersonal system. You'll avoid the pitfall of tools about which Henry David Thoreau warned us: becoming a tool of your tool.

This isn't so much about *reimagining* productivity as it is about *reclaiming* productivity. You start with redesigning what you need to truly be productive; then you rebuild your workflow to achieve those needs. As a result, you can reclaim productivity as it was intended.

There's no such thing as an app or a tool that everyone will use everywhere. Similarly, there's no such thing as a universal way of working and collaborating that everyone will use everywhere. It's crucial that you put a system in place that is simple, flexible, and durable enough to work with a variety of the apps, the tools, and the people with whom you'll work. Failing to do that means you will shortchange your productivity because you'll wind up working with a set of parameters that isn't made with you in mind.

> Remember that being productive isn't a one-and-done proposition. You can't turn it on and off like a faucet. Productivity is a lifestyle. It's a way of operating. Make your productivity system as ideal as you can for yourself. Because even though business isn't always personal, productivity always is.
>
> *Mike Vardy is a writer, productivity strategist, and the creator of the methodology and philosophy known as TimeCrafting. He is the author of several books, including the upcoming* TimeCrafting: A Better Way to Get the Right Things Done.

Multitasking

The popular term means concurrently doing a bunch of things. Multitaskers frequently switch between or among different tasks.

Neuroscientists and productivity experts reject the notion of *multitasking* because it actually hinders productivity. (For more on this subject, check out Mihaly Csikszentmihalyi's excellent 1990 book *Flow: The Psychology of Optimal Experience*.)

By extension, then, trying to simultaneously collaborate on too many projects is likely to detract from your team's performance—not to mention your own. What's more, your colleagues may come to resent you because you are dragging the team down with you.

Deep Work

College professor Cal Newport coined this popular phrase in his eponymous book *Deep Work: Rules for Focused Success in a Distracted World*.

At its core, deep work represents a period of time in which you accomplish your tasks in a focused and decidedly non-collaborative way. Even when you need to collaborate with others, it's best to unplug at times to focus on the critical task at hand.

Remote Work

You complete your tasks away from your employer's normal physical environment or office. Note that remote work may or may not involve collaboration.

Project Management

I've seen plenty of people conflate *collaboration* and *project management*. For several reasons, don't make this common mistake.

First, the term *project* connotes defined starting and end dates. Maybe your organization is implementing a new customer-relationship management system or running a client's marketing campaign. At some point, these projects will come to an end.

Second, project management doesn't necessarily need to be collaborative. For example, for years, Google famously allowed its engineers one day per week to independently pursue their own projects. In theory, this policy would yield innovations.

Communication in Action

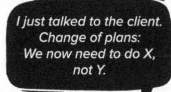

Cooperation in Action

Delegation in Action

Walter has left the company. Normally, I take care of X, but I need you to do it for me by this time and date.

I'm on it.

Coordination in Action

Got it.

I want to make sure that you're doing X in a manner that's consistent with that of everyone else on the team.

Productivity in Action

Multitasking in Action

Deep Work in Action

Remote Work in Action

Project Management in Action

The Limitations of Collaboration

For several reasons, it's essential to remember that collaboration is no superpower.

First, consider the following common business goals:

- Implementing a new salesforce-automation tool.
- Streamlining a business process.
- Launching a faster and more user-friendly mobile app.
- Reducing employee or customer turnover.

In each of these cases, would solid collaboration help the organization achieve its goal? No doubt, but there's no guarantee. Effective collaboration increases only the *chances* of a successful outcome.

Case in point: On August 24, 2020, OnwardMobility announced that it was working with BlackBerry to release new phones starting in 2021.[1] I have no doubt that these two organizations will try their hardest to resurrect the moribund brand. Things could go swimmingly well. Still, in all likelihood, the newfangled BlackBerry will fall flat on its face. (Other than IBM and Apple, name a tech company that has risen from the dead.)

Second, collaboration isn't a goal in and of itself. Plenty of individuals and teams work well together but fail to deliver results for one reason or another. Putting the adjective *remote* in front of *collaboration* only introduces new complexities.

A Simple Framework for Understanding Collaboration

All collaboration isn't created equal. Instead, it's instructive to think about collaboration across a number of key dimensions. Before we can reimagine it, we need to understand it.

Dimension #1: In Person vs. Remote

Where does the collaboration take place?

- **In Person:** Such collaboration involves working, brainstorming, and problem-solving with more than one person in the same physical space.
- **Remote:** This type of teamwork involves others who don't occupy the same physical space as you. By definition, this type of collaboration requires software and technology to bridge the gap.

Note that teams can collaborate in both physical and virtual environments. That is, hybrid approaches are possible, often advisable, and increasingly common. For example, it's usually best to hold difficult conversations or tackle thorny communication issues in person.

It's folly to think that all types of collaboration carry the same weight. As the following sidebar illustrates, that goes double when certain people are physically closer to key decision-makers.

Lack of Collaboration Helps Doom a Startup
Over my career, I have worked extensively with Eastern European technology teams. In 2018, a Manhattan-based cryptocurrency startup hired me as an independent consultant based upon my expertise.

By way of background, the execs and the product, sales, and marketing teams all operated out of Manhattan. The software developers, however, lived in Belarus, Brazil, and northern Canada. Although everyone used state-of-the-art videoconferencing and messaging technologies, communication and collaboration suffered from the get-go.

The team's vastly different time zones made synchronous communication challenging. Meetings usually occurred late in the day in New York—an inconvenient time for the developers. What's more, the fickle CEO would often cancel meetings and reschedule them for 10 p.m. his time. (That's 5 a.m. in Belarus.)

Invariably, the folks in New York exercised outsized influence on product-related decisions. The developers' lack of proximity to the action effectively marginalized them.

Ultimately, despite its innovative ideas, the startup failed for several reasons. First, as is often the case, its processes were too informal. For instance, no one documented decisions or formalized milestones. Second, its internal communication and collaboration were lacking. As a result, it couldn't respond rapidly enough to customer and investor requirements.

Jason Horowitz is an independent technology-strategy consultant.

Dimension #2: Synchronous vs. Asynchronous

All collaboration needs to take place in real time, right?

Nope.

Keith and Roger work as accountants for a consumer-products company. They frequently pop by each other's desks to investigate discrepancies or pick each other's brains about thorny issues. In the event that one of them is out, the other will leave a Post-it note or send an email with a Microsoft Excel workbook attachment asking for advice. In these cases, they are working together, but asynchronously.

Contrast that scenario with Mia and Vincent, two HR employees investigating potential executive misconduct during a recent company outing. For legal reasons, the pair needs to *concurrently* interview relevant parties to determine what happened. They want to know if senior executives behaved inappropriately. In this example, they are collaborating synchronously.

Synthesis

Put these two dimensions together, and you wind up with the following collaboration matrix:

The Dimensions of Collaboration

Synchronous

In-Person	Remote
Colleagues brainstorming ideas on a physical whiteboard	Colleagues collaborating in real time on a Google Doc
Union and management leadership negotiating at the bargaining table to reach a last-minute collective bargaining agreement	Client and agency employees brainstorming about the new marketing plan on a Zoom call
A team of paralegals reviewing paper documents as part of discovery for an upcoming case	Developers contributing to a code repository such as GitHub
Restaurant staff seating your family, preparing your meals, and serving you	A distributed team of data scientists is building an algorithm to predict customer behavior

Asynchronous

This figure represents my revised take on the computer-supported cooperative work (CSCW) first coined by Irene Greif and Paul M. Cashman way back in 1984.

FIGURE 2.1: The Dimensions of Collaboration

The examples in the preceding figure illustrate a number of key points:

- Certain types of collaboration need to take place synchronously and in person. A chef cannot virtually cook a meal. What's more, if she prepares Lobster Thermidor on Monday but the waiter serves it on Friday, customers may become ill.
- Some tasks, projects, and even entire professions lend themselves to collaboration more than others. In this vein, coders and data scientists are quite adept at using collaborative technologies to do their jobs. Doctors, university administrators, and mid-career government officials? Not so much.
- In some cases, individuals and teams can collaborate well in any manner they choose: synchronously or asynchronously, remotely or in person.

This begs an obvious question: How do you decide when collaboration should be remote or not—or synchronous vs. asynchronous?

What Type of Work Do You Do?

> "The mere consciousness of an engagement
> will sometimes worry a whole day."
> —CHARLES DICKENS

In July of 2009, legendary investor Paul Graham popularized a critical work-related distinction: Maker vs. Manager. From his influential blog post:

> In Manager Time, a day is neatly sliced up into hourly chunks according to the calendar. Meeting someone is as easy as finding a free slot that coincides. You don't have to worry too much about what you'll be doing next, as your calendar will tell you.
>
> In Maker Time, a day is an open book to get something hard and meaningful done. Even thinking when a meeting might be and remembering to go can distract from getting on with making. Long, uninterrupted chunks of time—not sliced and diced by meetings on the hour—are ideal to make progress on hard problems and tackle something new. Even a single meeting in the middle of an afternoon can disrupt that long meaningful chunk into two that make it harder to tackle something big as you have to context switch and pick up where you left off.[2]

The implications of Graham's distinction for collaboration are profound.

Managers tend to fill their days with attending meetings, sending emails, completing status reports, and performing other administrative tasks—*the activities that matter most to them*. In my consulting days, I often saw project managers call meetings essentially because they were bored. As such, these folks usually demand in-person, synchronous attention from others.

Conversely, creative folks consider these questionable supervisory activities a waste of time or even counterproductive. Graham's *makers* tend to despise meetings because they break their day's flow and prevent them from accomplishing their tasks.

Looking at Collaboration Through a Different Lens

Now put Graham's observations into the context of Figure 2.1. Equipped with your newfound lens, you can now identify the behaviors and activities that inhibit successful collaboration.

Consider the following scenarios.

Scenario A: Old Habits Die Hard

Samantha is an experienced project manager working with a team of three creatives on a marketing campaign. She insists upon holding daily 30-minute meetings at 11:30 a.m. She also peppers them throughout the day for updates on specific tasks, expecting immediate answers. (You may have seen this movie before.)

If you think that this situation does not represent the ideal way for everyone on the team to collaborate, trust your judgment.

While Samantha prefers this arrangement, the other creatives would benefit from communicating and collaborating in a fundamentally different way. Specifically, Samantha should hold group meetings earlier in the day. Doing so would allow the team members to focus on creative endeavors from that point forward.

Moreover, by relying upon email, she's committing two cardinal communication and collaboration sins. First, her messages lack valuable context. After all, anyone can email you about anything.

Second, she's maximizing the chance that those emails will distract her teammates. That is, the others will see messages containing important news and tasks from others. To improve the team's collaboration, Samantha should move all of the team's text-based communication to an internal collaboration hub, such as Slack or Microsoft Teams. Both allow people to customize notifications in a way that Outlook and Gmail simply cannot.

Scenario B: Fear of In-Person Contact

Jerry, Elaine, Kramer, and George work as managers at a large regional bank. They are concerned about the recent rise in refinance applications and how to respond to this trend.

Because they are so busy, the four eschew proper meetings. In their place, they use Microsoft Teams to exchange asynchronous messages throughout the day. They also send drafts of plans back and forth.

No worries here, right?

Wrong.

The team is relying too heavily upon asynchronous collaboration—and Microsoft Teams in particular. At some point, the four of them should meet in person to flush out the financial arcana. Fortunately, they can keep using Teams. It is more than capable of hosting multi-person videoconference calls.

Chapter Summary

- Don't confuse collaboration with adjacent work-related terms.
- Collaboration isn't a superpower. Putting the adjective *remote* in front of it only makes it more difficult to attain.
- Contemporary collaboration is multidimensional. One size doesn't fit all. As such, doing it well is far easier said than done.

chapter 3

The Benefits of Reimagining Collaboration

"No one can whistle a symphony.
It takes a whole orchestra to play it."

—H.E. LUCCOCK

The core premise of this book is that most businessfolks aren't communicating and collaborating effectively—at least to the extent possible. New technologies by themselves won't get us home.

By adopting a new model of collaboration and a new mindset, organizations, departments, groups, and individual employees can realize significant advantages.

But which ones?

This chapter answers that question in spades.

Increase Organizational and Group Transparency

Imagine if Enron's employees had known that the house of cards was about to come crashing down. Many of them would have changed jobs—or at least reallocated the holdings in their retirement accounts before the company spectacularly imploded.

Knowing what's going on at work is fundamental. After all, who wants to be kept in the dark?

In October of 2018, Slack published the results of a study conducted by the consumer-insights and strategy-consulting firm Kelton Global.[1] KG surveyed more than 1,400 knowledge workers across the U.S., 500 of whom used Slack.

Among KG's most interesting findings:

- 87 percent of workers want their future company to be transparent.
- 80 percent are interested in discovering more about how their organization makes decisions.
- 55 percent of business owners described their organization as "very transparent," but only 18 percent of their employees agreed with that assessment.

Used properly, collaboration hubs can promote organizational, department, and group transparency. But the benefits don't stop there.

Amplify the Flow of Knowledge Throughout the Organization

There's a surfeit of research on how new technologies facilitate knowledge sharing within groups and organizations. That's great, but what are the specific benefits that knowledge transfer confers?

Let's start with productivity.

The Technology Services Industry Association found that nearly three in four companies anticipate that they can increase productivity by at least 20 percent if they improved how they manage institutional knowledge.[2]

Beyond making employees more productive, however, sharing knowledge can result in:

- Better business decisions.
- More efficient business processes, as I'll discuss in Chapter 10.
- Greater collaboration.
- Improved professional relationships.

Not too shabby.

Boost Team and Organizational Productivity

I'm not finished with productivity. Today's breed of powerful collaboration tools allows organizations, departments, teams, and even individuals to increase their productivity. It's that simple, but don't take my word for it.

The market-research outfit Forrester studied the benefits that organizations can expect to realize by using today's proper collaboration hubs. Among the major findings of its September 2020 report, applications such as Slack:

> . . . eliminated significant friction in communications due to its ability to organize information into relevant channels, searchable history, and support for both synchronous and asynchronous communication.[3]

If teams are more productive, then it stands to reason that organizations will be as well. But how, exactly, do collaborative tools make employees more productive?

Waste Less Employee Time

At work, people generate an enormous amount of content—much of which they can't find easily or even at all. I'm talking about Excel spreadsheets, PowerPoint presentations, contracts in Word, and other key documents.

As I cover in Chapter 4, workers who rely upon email frequently struggle to find key messages in their bloated inboxes. The Findwise 2016 Enterprise Search & Findability survey found that a full one-third of employees experienced problems finding basic information.[4] Ouch.

What to do?

Software vendors long ago recognized the simple yet massive opportunity of helping employees find key files. To wit, an entire category of software purports to solve this vexing problem. In basic terms, *enterprise search and retrieval* applications allow workers to more quickly locate content while on the clock. And this is no niche market. In late 2016, Grand View Research estimated that the ESR industry will reach nearly $9 billion by 2024.

For two reasons, people who use collaborative hubs as central knowledge repositories waste less time trying to locate files, decisions, and conversations. First, they need to look in only one application. Second, these tools offer powerful search functionality.

Less time searching for key files and information means less frustration and greater efficiency.

Be a Healthier and More Profitable Organization

Is your organization healthy? And how would you know?

These two simple questions are tough for most folks to answer when everyone works under the same roof, let alone when remote work is the norm.

Consider 2017 research by the venerable management consulting firm McKinsey. Its leadership conducted a study titled "Organizational health: A fast track to performance improvement." It defined *strong organizational health* as "the ability to rally around a common vision, execute effectively, and create a culture of innovation."[5]

I'll cut to the chase: Organizations that exhibited this characteristic delivered roughly three times better returns to their shareholders than those that didn't.

No, there's no cause-and-effect relationship between organizational health and collaboration. Allow me to present a counterfactual, though: Think about a company whose employees don't collaborate well. Is it likely to be a healthy and profitable one?

> **All else being equal, a healthy, transparent, and collaborative organization is more likely to be a profitable one.**

Identify Organizational Blind Spots and Vulnerabilities

Think about a key skill that all employees in your organization need to possess. Examples include common sense, communication, and basic civility. No, not everyone needs to be Dale Carnegie in the office, but outrightly rude folks cast a pall over the workplace. These cancers poison the well for others. In the extreme, they expose their employer to lawsuits.

Add effective collaboration to the list of equally critical requirements. A single recalcitrant group or employee can gum up the works for everyone else.

Fortunately, a transparent, healthy, and truly collaborative organization is better equipped to identify problematic folks, remedy their behavior, and remove them if all else fails. Put simply, it's easier to spot these outliers. (Chapter 11 covers problematic employees and how to handle them.)

Other Benefits

Effective collaboration can confer a number of other significant benefits. All else being equal, organizations that collaborate well are more likely to:

- **Retain customers.** Few things irritate people more than playing dial-a-rep. For example, you have to call a 1-800 number and explain the same thing over and over again because a company's reps aren't communicating or collaborating well.
- **Build trust among employees.** For more than three decades, online communities have allowed others to connect across the globe. Similarly, collaborative tools can foster a sense of community among people, regardless of where they are.
- **Retain employees.** People leave their jobs for all sorts of reasons. The company whose employees collaborate well eliminates one of them.
- **Communicate better.** As mentioned in Chapter 2, communication and collaboration are cousins. By definition, teams that collaborate well are less likely to drop the ball because of misunderstandings.

Chapter Summary

- If you think that collaboration is an elixir, you're bound to be disappointed.

- Effective collaboration allows organizations to become more transparent, healthier, and less-stressful places to work.
- Firms and teams that collaborate well will be more productive than their collaboration-challenged counterparts.

Chapter 4

Why Email Inhibits Collaboration

"Yeah. Uh, did you get that memo?"
—GARY COLE AS BILL LUMBERGH, *Office Space*

For the last two decades, I have advocated using collaborative technologies in the workplace in lieu of email. I can report a number of little victories and even a few big ones. Unfortunately, often my collaboration suggestions to clients, colleagues, and superiors, and partners have fallen on deaf ears.

The reasons varied, but my two most formidable obstacles were others' beliefs that:

- Sending a message was the same as holding an actual conversation.
- The medium for sending that message didn't matter.

I call bullshit on both.

At best, people who rely upon Microsoft Outlook or Gmail to "collaborate" introduce superfluous friction. They make it harder for themselves and others to effectively work together. The word *suboptimal* readily comes to mind. Often, they make collaboration downright impossible.

In this chapter, I'll list five of the reasons that email inhibits effective collaboration.

Email Wasn't Designed for Collaboration

Email allows just about anyone in the world to contact you—and vice versa. In fancier terms, email benefits from a powerful *network effect*. Much like social networks, landlines in the 20th century, and other mass-communication tools, its immense value stems from its near ubiquity.

> **Paradoxically, email's greatest strength in one important but limited context is its greatest weakness in all others.**

Let me explain.

Email is effectively universal. Precisely because of that, just about anyone can contact you about anything. In the process, their messages appear at the top of your *de facto* to-do list. Make no mistake: This is a feature of email, not a bug.[*] For this very reason, email has served as an indispensable tool for business communication for the last 25 years.

Remember from Chapter 2, though, that it's dangerous to conflate communication with collaboration, productivity,

---

[*] Interestingly, Basecamp's new Hey email service solves this very problem through a powerful whitelist.

and other work-related terms. And here's where email's utility wanes.

Using a vanilla inbox to manage your communication just doesn't work. Fine, but what about filters, rules, anti-spam protection, blacklists, tags, whitelists, and other Band-Aids? And what about productivity philosophies such as Inbox Zero?

Sure, they can help. But even the most advanced email hacks and systems don't change the simple, immutable fact that email was never designed for collaboration.

Email Fails to Capture Essential Organizational Knowledge

Contrary to what many people think, all text-based communications are not created equal. Where any given message ultimately "lives" matters much more than most people realize.

Individual inboxes effectively die when employees leave the company.

Let that sink in for a moment.

Sure, many or even most of your emails might be irrelevant or, at least, not terribly important. Let's say that four in five of your messages consist of the following:

- Company announcements.
- Notes from overly solicitous vendors.
- Reminders or nastygrams from HR or your manager.
- Colleagues' auto-responses and general bloviating.

As such, these emails don't contain particularly valuable information.

Fair enough, but what about that other 20 percent?

I'm willing to bet that, over the course of your career, you have sent and received plenty of sensitive emails about key company, department, or group issues. Maybe you've chimed in with a concern about a colleague or dangerous trend. People use email every day—myriad times—to do these very things.

These decisions, communications, and concerns aren't for public consumption. (Would you have sent them otherwise?) Still, should those organizational or group messages disappear just because the people on the email thread have left their jobs?

Absolutely not. That knowledge is far too valuable to let it vanish for good.

In rare cases and when directed, an employee in the IT department can resurrect an employee's email account to locate a key piece of information. Alternatively, lawsuits often involve subpoenas demanding access to internal correspondence. In either event, it takes additional resources and effort to find the needle in a haystack of tens or even hundreds of thousands of employee emails. What's more, success is anything but guaranteed.

Email Provides Only One Bite at the Apple

I have known for decades that email is a scourge. I didn't realize the extent of the problem until 2014. I was researching my book *Message Not Received: Why Business Communication Is Broken and How to Fix It.*

It's not uncommon for knowledge workers to spend 25 to 30 percent of their days in their inboxes.[1] That equates to two hours per day—every day.

With so much time spent sending emails, you're bound to make a mistake from time to time. We all do. Specific gaffes run the gamut:

- Replying to all when you meant to reply to the sender.
- Using regrettable language.
- Failing to attach a file to a message.
- More innocuously, sending a message with a typo or misspelled word.

Most mainstream email programs allow users to undo or recall sending a message, but these are sketchy propositions. Maybe it works; maybe it doesn't. (In case of emergencies, we might dial the help desk and plead that someone in IT intervene to prevent a disaster.)

When we catch our own mistakes, we reply to our own emails by including the intended attachment or apologizing for our blunder. When we don't, someone else needs to respond to our emails requesting clarification.

Brass tacks: Once you hit "Send," your message is broadcast for all recipients to see—warts and all.

Contrast email with internal collaboration hubs. They allow users to easily edit and delete messages *after sending them*. For example, if you spot your typo two days later, then just fix it—without peppering the group with additional messages. The end result: fewer messages for everyone.

Can anyone argue with receiving fewer messages?

No, like email, Slack, Zoom, and Microsoft Teams don't allow you to wipe a colleague's memory if he reads something that you sent in error. If Derek sees your inflammatory message, you still will pay the piper. Regardless, these collaboration hubs offer far better functionality compared to email. It's not even close.

Emails Lack Critical Context

We've all felt overwhelmed at work at one point or another. Working remotely has certainly conferred benefits—most notably, saying *adios* to our long daily commutes. In a critical way, however, nothing has changed: Employees continue to juggle multiple projects, and a deluge of messages. Plus, we now have to deal with the new phenomenon of Zoom fatigue.

A more formal term for "taxing your working memory" is *cognitive load*. The American Psychological Association defines it as "the relative demand imposed by a particular task, in terms of mental resources required."[2] In layman's terms, our ability to concentrate is limited. Over the course of the day, we deplete our available mental energy.

But what does all of this have to do with email?

Plenty.

Every time you check your inbox, you're tapping into that finite pool of mental energy. When you receive a new message, it might take you only a second or two to determine who sent it and what it's about. Remember: By definition, emails can essentially come from anyone in the world about any subject. And they don't have to be even remotely relevant.

Over the course of the day, however, those precious seconds add up. More than time, however, your brain devotes some of its critical and finite capacity to *repeatedly* answering a number of simple questions:

1. Who sent me this message?
2. Is it relevant to me?
3. What's it about? (Something that the subject line doesn't necessarily manifest.)
4. What, if anything, do I need to do about it?
5. When do I need to do it?

Imagine asking yourself those questions 100 times per day—every day. Put bluntly, email often lacks valuable context.

Contrast email with contemporary collaboration hubs. For example, say that you work at a law firm. Employees use a dedicated Slack workspace for internal communication and collaboration. The workspace consists of different subject-specific *channels*. Think of them as virtual meeting rooms in which people discuss individual subjects. A channel is the antithesis of a one-size-fits-all inbox.

Slack notifies you of a new message in the `legal_affairs` channel. You are immediately aware that a colleague has posted a question or note *about that specific topic*. You don't know exactly what, but at least you've got a general idea. You don't need to ask yourself those same five questions. Translation: Your brain saves previous energy, and you reduce your cognitive load.

If you're still not sold on the import of saving mental energy, consider the following sidebar.

> ## *Why e-Commerce Companies Obsess Over Simplicity*
>
> The most successful e-commerce players have long understood the importance of reducing customers' cognitive load. Put bluntly, less friction helps the bottom line.
>
> Confusing websites and laborious check-out processes add friction and deter customers from ultimately making purchases. As a result, sales suffer. Providing relevant context and making things simple isn't just wise. It's required.*

Email Notifications Are Binary

Filters and rules aside, an inbox displays one daunting number: Unread messages. In this way, Outlook and Gmail treat a key response or note from your boss the same as just another irrelevant reminder or nastygram.

Contrast email programs with the internal collaboration hubs detailed in the next chapter. Night and day. The latter allow for a remarkable level of alert customization.

If Not Email, Then What?

Say that powerful, affordable, and user-friendly alternatives to email didn't exist. If that were true, then none of its core limitations would be as galling, obvious, and frustrating as they are.

---

* For more on this subject, check out Steve Krug's excellent book *Don't Make Me Think: A Common Sense Approach to Web Usability.*

Fortunately, fundamentally better communication and collaboration tools have existed for years—and that is the subject of Part II.

Chapter Summary

●——● Email was never designed for collaboration. Despite its limitations, many people tolerated it because of inertia and the lack of viable collaboration alternatives.

●——● Employees have traditionally stored essential knowledge, decisions, and information in their inboxes—all of which effectively disappear when they leave their jobs.

●——● Over the course of a day, email saps your brain to an extent that modern collaboration tools do not.

Part II

Better Collaboration
Through Technology

chapter 5

Reimagining Workplace Technology

"Man is a tool-using animal.
Without tools, he is nothing; with tools he is all."
—THOMAS CARLYLE

People of a certain age remember that rudimentary communication and collaboration tools arrived during the nascent days of the Web. Early entrants included a slew of applications based upon the Internet Relay Chat protocol. In fact, hardcore techies from back in the day argue that the same fundamental structure exists in most of today's internal collaboration hubs. They're not totally wrong.

Over the past 30 years, though, the applications that allow us to exchange information and work together have become far more powerful than their antecedents. The word *supercharged* readily comes to mind.

This trend has not gone unnoticed. The market for collaboration software was *already* exploding in popularity before we started wearing masks in public. In late 2019, the prominent research firm Gartner predicted that worldwide revenue from collaboration software would nearly double by 2023.[1] Its analysts surmised that the market would grow from an estimated $2.7 billion in 2018 to $4.8 billion by 2023, nearly doubling in size.

And that was before the greatest work-from-home experiment in the history of the world began.

A Few Disclaimers

Whether collaboration should happen in person or remotely is ultimately moot. More and more of it is becoming remote—a trend that will only continue with the arrival of COVID-19 vaccinations.

Against this backdrop, it's hard to overstate the heightened importance of effective collaboration. New applications play an essential role in achieving this worthy and often-elusive goal.

Despite collaboration tools' immense power and utility, I'll be the first to admit that, by themselves, they are not panaceas. They do not magically fix dysfunctional cultures, nor will they resurrect failing companies. Claiming otherwise would be downright irresponsible.

Defining Key Terms

At the core of this book is a new model of collaboration and work. Before introducing it, it's imperative to define two key terms:

- **Internal collaboration hub:** A general-use software application designed to promote effective internal communication and collaboration. Ideally, hubs consist of all organizational conversations, decisions, documents, and institutional knowledge. Critically, hubs connect to spokes. They enable automation in ways that require little-to-no technical skill.
- **Spoke:** A software application designed for a specific purpose, such as productivity, content creation, customer-relationship management, and project management. Spokes connect to hubs. As a result, employee, group, department, and organizational communication and collaboration markedly improve.

Today's Most Popular Collaboration Hubs

Although their adoption is far from universal,* internal collaboration hubs have become all the rage. (As discussed in Chapter 1, COVID-19 didn't start this trend; it accelerated an existing one.) In that vein, it's time to briefly introduce the most popular players in the workplace-collaboration market.

---

* See Fubini's Law in the Introduction.

The Big Three

As of this writing, three companies' hubs dominate the market. In terms of numbers of users and influence, the following vendors stand heads and shoulders above their peers.

Slack

Formerly an online game called *Glitch*, Slack launched in August of 2013. Its quirky name stands for *Searchable Log of All Communication and Knowledge*. Sure, it's a backronym, but don't let its contrived name and slacker connotation fool you. Slack is an incredibly powerful and user-friendly tool. For this very reason, a few tech titans attempted to acquire it before it went public.[2] As of this writing, more than 12 million daily active users find Slack indispensable.[3] I proudly put myself in that camp. (In December of 2020, Salesforce announced that it was acquiring Slack for $28 billion.)

Microsoft Teams

One of Slack's would-be early suitors was Microsoft—hardly a stranger to collaboration software. Over the years, Microsoft has launched or acquired a swath of applications that allows people to effectively share information and work together. Its current properties include Yammer, SharePoint, the consumer *and* business versions of Skype,[*] and its most recent baby, Microsoft Teams. (No, Outlook doesn't count.)

Launched in 2017, Teams feels like a more formal version of Slack—and that's no accident. Because Microsoft plays in so

---

[*] Microsoft has announced that it will be retiring Skype for Business on July 31, 2021. For more on this, see https://bit.ly/nog-skype.

many different markets, it typically adopts a fast-follower strategy with many of its products, including and especially Teams.
Put differently, Teams eventually apes most of its competitors'
popular features once they have demonstrated their value.

Microsoft controversially bundles Teams with its nearly
ubiquitous Office 365 suite, making it effectively free for all
organizations that pay for Microsoft Word, Excel, Outlook,
and PowerPoint licenses.*

Zoom

At the end of 2019, you probably hadn't heard of Zoom.
At that time, 10 million primarily enterprise customers happily
used it for videoconferencing. During the pandemic, Zoom's
user base exploded, as Figure 5.1 shows. It became the *de
facto* videoconferencing standard.[4]

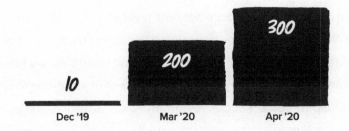

Zoom's Insane User Growth

Daily Active Users (in Millions)

300

200

10

Dec '19   Mar '20   Apr '20

Source: *The Verge, Zoom.*

FIGURE 5.1: Zoom's Insane User Growth

---

* Whether Microsoft will be able to continue doing this is anyone's
  guess. Slack filed a claim in July of 2020 with the European Union
  claiming that this practice is illegal. Many U.S. scholars believe
  that antitrust laws are long overdue for an overhaul.

Zoom won't say, but I'd wager that at least 80 percent of its customers use it exclusively for holding video calls. (This is its Meetings & Chat tool.) In point of fact, Zoom's increasingly robust collaboration functionality includes many of the same features in Slack and Microsoft Teams.

Along with its user base, Zoom's market capitalization has ballooned by more than an order of magnitude since late 2019. As a result, it can acquire competitors whose products offer new, valuable, and complementary features.

The Others

While not quite as prominent as the prior three, other software vendors are attempting to catch up—most with very deep pockets. For different reasons, however, they trail the pack as of this writing.

Workplace from Facebook

Yet another entrant into this crowded space is Workplace from Facebook. The social network's value proposition is simple: Workplace requires no training because so many people already use Facebook. Spotify, Petco, and Nestle all pay Mark Zuckerberg's company for the privilege of using Workplace.

Despite some successes, many CIOs and IT managers are reluctant to trust Facebook with their sensitive enterprise information—and for good reason. The social network's track record on privacy and security is disgraceful.*

---

* Read *Zucked: Waking Up to the Facebook Catastrophe* by early Facebook investor Roger McNamee if you don't believe me.

Google Workspace

Like Microsoft, Google's different communication and collaboration offerings have overlapped and often baffled users.[5] Its tools have previously included Meet, Hangouts, Duo, and Voice. Today, Google is pushing Chat as part of its Workspace suite that includes the popular tools Gmail, Docs, Drive, Calendar, Meet, and more.

Cisco Webex Teams

No one would confuse it with the sexier and vastly more popular Zoom, but it's a mistake to ignore Cisco's Webex Teams. At a high level, it allows employees to send messages, share files, call their peers, brainstorm, and take notes on virtual whiteboards.

Put mildly, the Webex brand has faded over time. These days, sending people a Webex link is akin to using an *aol.com* email address.

Discord

Discord is a bit different from the other collaboration hubs mentioned in this section. Yes, it operates under the freemium business model, but it's an open-source project. This means that developers can legally fork it*, and some have. Second, it is more of a gaming and social tool. That's not to say, however, that many professional groups don't use it to collaborate and exchange information.

---

* In short, developers can create their own versions of it and release them into the wild.

Why Today's Hubs Destroy Email and Their Predecessors

To be sure, ephemeral differences persist among these collaboration applications. To say that one of the applications discussed in this chapter is "the best" is foolish.

> ## Fast Followers
>
> Slack, Google, Zoom, Microsoft, and the other major players pay close attention to what the rest of them are doing. A neat feature that differentiates one vendor's wares can become table stakes in a few months. As a result, their bells and whistles are converging. MBA types will correctly recognize the *fast-follower strategy* in action.
>
> It's never been tougher to build moats around software applications. It's fair to call the similarities around today's internal collaboration hubs *remarkable*.

If you want to collaborate effectively with others, each of these tools decimates email. It's not even close.*

Here's why.

Better All-Around Context

Chapter 4 describes how email induces cognitive load. By providing far more context to each message, collaboration hubs minimize this issue. Your brain will notice the difference.

---

* To watch a webinar on the major features of today's main collaboration hubs, see https://bit.ly/nog-web.

Modern Design and Ease of Use

Odds are that you're familiar with the conventions of social networks. I'm talking about the @ and # symbols, respectively. Slack, Microsoft Teams, and other hubs incorporate these features in ways that have become natural to us over the past decade. The end result: At least for understanding the basics of each application, you'll be up and running in no time.

Integrations With Other Essential Systems and Applications

Unlike their predecessors, modern collaboration hubs don't exist in a vacuum. On the contrary, they play nicely with a wide array of third-party apps. To use a fifty-cent word, they are more *extensible*.

> ### How the Magic Happens
>
> Three powerful tools allow developers to extend the native power of today's internal collaboration hubs. Collectively, these mechanisms allow different applications and services to seamlessly integrate with others.
>
> Of course, end users need not know any of these technical underpinnings to take advantage of their immense power. And you certainly don't need to know how to code.
>
> - **Application programming interfaces (APIs):** An API acts as a sort of software intermediary. It allows two applications to effectively talk to each

other. A vendor's API typically serves as a primary access point for interactions with third-party apps.

- **Webhooks:** At a high level, webhooks are automated messages sent from apps after an event takes place. Software developers use them to do a number of really cool things under the hood.
- **Software development kits (SDKs):** At their core, SDKs allow developers to easily create powerful new applications. Through SDKs, developers can create iOS, MacOS, iPadOS, Android, and Windows apps.

Cost and Affordability

Over the last 20 years, most legacy software vendors have shifted their business models from traditional, one-time purchases to recurring subscriptions. Today, software-as-a-service (SaaS) is the default *modus operandi* for thousands of outfits, including Zoom, Slack, and Microsoft. While everyday employees may not have noticed the move to SaaS, the implications for corporate accounting and finance are profound.

SaaS means that organizations usually pay for software by the month. In terms of contracts, think Netflix, not Verizon or AT&T. A CIO no longer needs to argue for a massive one-time capital expenditure. These lower operational expenses are far easier to digest. Beyond the financial implications, however, firms no longer fear vendor lock-in—at least to the same degree. That is, they can more easily switch to new tools without succumbing to the sunk-cost fallacy.*

Versatility

These hubs' technological building blocks usually overlap. Users typically benefit from dedicated channels, direct messages, and the other features described in this section. As you'll quickly discover, though, today's internal collaboration hubs are remarkably protean.

The next chapter delves deeper into this subject. For now, suffice it to say that it's easy to both customize and connect them to a wide variety of internal systems and applications.

Knowledge Management

Used properly, an internal collaboration hub represents a single, robust source of information and knowledge. It serves as valuable and permanent knowledge repository that survives even when employees leave their jobs for greener pastures.

Superior Search

When people use collaboration hubs, they spend far less time looking for key documents. Make no mistake: These savings add up.

---

* People are often loath to reverse bad decisions, even when they cannot recover their costs. An economist will tell you that you should leave a movie if it sucks because you can get your time back, if not your money.

Smartphones and Portability

Say goodbye to the days of needing to use a proper computer to work with your colleages. Each of the hubs in this chapter ships with a robust and user-friendly mobile app.

More Robust and Customizable Notifications

Smartphones and apps are mixed blessings. Without self-control, they can become electronic leashes. Fortunately, these hubs allow users to easily activate Do-Not-Disturb mode. Also, by keeping all internal communications in Zoom or Slack, you minimize the risk of checking your email and getting sucked into work matters while on the golf course or the beach.

Automation

Hubs allow us to automate an increasing number of tasks. I could cite dozens of examples of how they minimize manual work and data entry. Here's one. A training manager creates recurring announcements, updates, and messages. As a result, she doesn't need to manually create and send quarterly emails.

Benjamin Button

I've saved the best for last.

The minute you drive your newly purchased car off the lot, its value decreases. Within a month, even if you keep it in your garage, it's probably worth ten percent less than what you paid for it.[6]

By contrast, consider some of the most successful companies over the last fifteen years: Amazon, Facebook, Google, and Netflix. These companies' algorithms become *more* predictive, powerful, and valuable over time. NYU marketing professor and serial entrepreneur Scott Galloway* has termed this *the Benjamin Button Economy*—a reference to Brad Pitt's eponymous character in the 2008 film.[7]

Internal collaboration hubs work the same way: They become *more* valuable over time. In other words, they age in reverse.

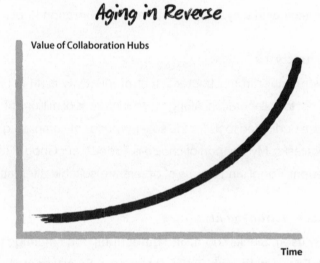

Aging in Reverse

Value of Collaboration Hubs

Time

FIGURE 5.2: Aging in Reverse

Complementary Software Applications

Hubs such as Slack, Microsoft Teams, and Zoom allow people to work together in a far more fluid fashion than email ever

---

* When I rock my black glasses, I become his doppelgänger. We both have written popular books about Amazon, Apple, Facebook, and Google. I like mine, but his is better.

could. Still, by themselves, they don't eliminate our need to use other essential software applications. Put differently, Zoom is not a project-management tool. No one should confuse it with a proper productivity-tracking application. The smartest of cookies can't use Microsoft Teams to run a company's payroll or manage its supply chain.

The following complementary tools don't fall under the collaboration umbrella, *per se*. In this book, I refer to them as *spokes*. Effective collaboration today requires using them, increasingly in ways tied to internal collaboration hubs.

Productivity

Remember from Chapter 2 that productivity is an adjacent concept to collaboration. Along these lines, tens of millions of people use dedicated tools for the sole purposes of completing *individual* tasks. My weapon of choice is Todoist, but Google Tasks, Freedom, Toggl, and scores of others are suitable alternatives.

Project Management

By itself, Slack, Zoom, and other hubs don't manage projects. Fear not, though. Trello, Basecamp, Smartsheet, Asana, Wrike, and others are more than capable of handling massive, multi-person projects.

Content Creation

Odds are that you're already familiar with Google's Workspace, formerly G Suite. For my money, it represents the best array of group-productivity tools. Expect Microsoft Office to launch many Workspace features over the coming years.

A relative newcomer is Dropbox. The online file-storage trailblazer joined the fray on June 16, 2019.[8] Its management decided that focusing purely on file storage didn't hold as much long-term promise.

Enterprise Systems

While not terribly sexy, organizations could not function properly without back- and front-office systems. I'm talking about software to help manage customers, the supply chain, financial transactions, HR and payroll, and the like.

Chapter Summary

- The market for collaboration tools was exploding long before people began wearing masks in public.
- Today's collaboration hubs are far more powerful, affordable, extensible, and user-friendly than their predecessors.
- Even the best collaboration hubs don't replicate the functionality of dedicated productivity, project-management, and enterprise systems.

Chapter 6

The Hub-Spoke Model of Collaboration

> *"Essentially, all models are wrong,*
> *but some are useful."*
> —GEORGE E. P. BOX

Consider two companies of equal size, age, and profitability: ABC and XYZ.

People at ABC rely upon a torrent of emails and attachments to exchange information and "collaborate." Its business processes haven't changed in 30 years. Employees are stuck in their ways. On the other hand, XYZ's culture is very different. Everyone uses Slack; it's the default medium for internal communication.

Without any other information, which sounds like the more collaborative work environment?

It's not even close.

Confusion most likely rules the day at ABC. Projects take longer to complete. Inefficiency is rampant. For its part, I'd wager that XYZ employees are far more likely to effectively collaborate—both in person and remotely.

In the example above, I intentionally painted a false dichotomy: One company embraced a proper collaboration hub, while the other did not. In fact, however, use of these hubs—and collaboration in general—is *not* binary. There are degrees. Many organizations, groups, and individuals use Microsoft Teams, Slack, and Zoom to a limited extent. They are merely scratching the surface.

It doesn't have to be this way. In this chapter, I'll explain how new technologies can boost collaboration throughout your team, department, and organization.

Why We Use Multiple Applications— and Always Will

On any given day and depending on your role, you probably use at least ten software programs, apps, or websites at work. The odds that you use only one or two are remote. As the following sidebar illustrates, even small businesses today rely upon a wide array of technologies.

Small Company. Many Tools.

Jay Baer is the founder of Convince & Convert Consulting, a digital marketing and customer experience advisory firm that helps Oracle, Cisco, Nike, and many other iconic brands. Much like Basecamp and Automattic, Baer's 15-employee company has been remote since it started in 2008. As such, powerful collaboration technologies have been essential to its success.

In October of 2020, Baer appeared as a guest on my podcast *Conversations About Collaboration*.[1] During our discussion, he revealed that Convince & Convert currently subscribes to 75 different software services. Among the three most useful:

- **Sucoco:** Software that lets employees work remotely side by side.
- **Vidyard:** A tool for creating and sharing quick videos, not unlike Loom.
- **Teamwork:** A project-management application.

Let's just say that I can relate to using many different tools.

At the far end of the spectrum, the typical freelancer or independent contractor uses quite a few applications—far more than if she had worked for a company as a full-time employee. In my case, the most popular arrows in my current quiver include:

- Slack, Zoom, and Microsoft Teams for collaboration and videoconferencing with my clients and vendors. (I'll explain why I use them all shortly.)
- Most of the Microsoft Office applications, especially Word when I'm working on the manuscript for a book.
- Google Workspace for creating documents that I intend to share with others.
- Safari and Brave to browse the web.
- The graphics-creation tool Canva.

- Basecamp, Asana, and Trello for project management.
- WaveApps for my accounting[*].
- LinkedIn and Twitter for social networking.
- Todoist to complete tasks and track my productivity.
- Tableau to create interactive data visualizations.
- WordPress for managing my website and blogging.
- Atom and CodePen for writing and testing code.
- OneDrive and Dropbox to back up and share large files[†].
- PDFPen to edit PDFs and sign contracts.
- Feedly and Pocket for feeding my brain and keeping up on current events.
- iMovie and Wave.video for creating and editing videos.
- GarageBand for creating and editing podcasts.
- Dashlane for password management.
- And probably twenty other software applications for professional and personal use.

I'm not bragging. Really. Trust me: I can cite a much longer list of technologies that I *don't* use in any given week or have never used at all. The Adobe Creative Cloud, most proper customer-relationship management and enterprise-resource-planning systems, web-development frameworks, and plenty of others come to mind.

The Method to My Madness

As an independent speaker, consultant, and trainer, I work with different organizations and people in a variety

---

[*] I only wish that I'd known about this tool years ago.
[†] I prefer to insert links to files in my emails instead of attachments.

of capacities. I have to adapt to my clients' needs. For example, one of my publishers uses Microsoft Teams. I can't very well force my editor to use Slack because it's my preference. Even I am not that unreasonable.

Next, I deliberately use certain best-of-breed tools over ones that large software vendors clearly consider afterthoughts. Generally speaking, the former are so much richer and powerful than the latter. Case in point: When it comes to productivity and task management, Microsoft To Do can't hold a candle to Todoist.

Third, and as I'll explain later in this chapter, I stitch as many of these applications together as possible. In the process, I minimize or eliminate tedium: duplicate data entry, manual work, and setting unnecessary reminders.

I also don't employ a proper staff. If I did, then my use of many apps would attenuate. Case in point: An accountant would handle my books for me.

Finally, I abide by the following maxim: Trying to cram all of your digital activities into a single application or two—no matter how robust—is a fool's errand.

This tool jockey isn't delusional—*at least not entirely*. The person who uses the most technology doesn't win. Still, we need different applications. No one should ever use a project-management tool to brainstorm. A dedicated mind-mapping app or physical whiteboard is far more suitable. By the same token, don't try to use a simple Google Doc to manage the multi-million-dollar launch of a new enterprise system.

Depending on your role, you will use plenty of different software applications. That thought might be harrowing. Fortunately, it is relatively easy to stitch these disparate tools together in a user-friendly and holistic manner—one that promotes effective collaboration.

A Simple Framework for Promoting Collaboration

In the previous chapter, I referred to Slack, Zoom, Microsoft Teams, and their ilk as *internal collaboration hubs*. I chose the term *hubs* deliberately because those tools allow people to easily connect to a wide variety of different applications that I call *spokes*.

Put differently, hubs act as the home base for an organization, a department, a team, and even an individual employee.

Figure 6.1 on the next page shows a visual.

Hubs provide an unprecedented level of integration among disparate programs, systems, and tools.[*]

Figure 6.1 is useful as a general construct, but does it reflect reality?

In short, yes. Here is how one of today's major software vendors is betting its future on this very model.

During its 2020 Zoomtopia conference (held virtually, of course), Zoom announced an impressive array of third-party apps or *Zapps*. By the time you read these words, users will access other tools *while in Zoom*.[2] In other words, other apps will live on top of Zoom; Zoom is the hub that connects the spokes. Figure 6.2 shows the user interface of the new Zoom:

---

[*] The technical, clunky term here is *interoperability*.

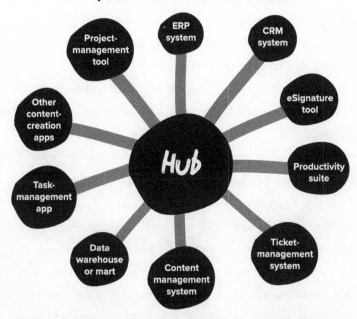

FIGURE 6.1: The Hub-Spoke Model of Collaboration

FIGURE 6.2: Zoom Zapps

Lest you think that this is the crazy vision of one company, it is not. During Slack's annual Frontiers conference in October of 2020, its leadership laid out an eerily similar vision for the future of work.* Don't think that Microsoft, Google, and other software vendors weren't paying close attention.

As I explain in the following sidebar, think of all other software applications as spokes that connect to the main hub.

The Hub-Spoke Model in Action

Consider Cygnus,† a hypothetical widget maker. Alex, Geddy, and Neil all work in the sales department. The three of them are devising next year's strategic plan.

Let's say that Neil creates the plan as a Google Doc. Alex comments on it. Neil can certainly receive that notification as a traditional email. With a few clicks of the mouse, though, he can opt to receive those alerts in Slack instead. Alternatively, if Geddy accidentally sends him an email, he can forward that message into Slack and continue the conversation there.

But we're just getting started.

Cygnus pipes customer leads from its website into Salesforce, its customer-relationship management system. This automatically creates a record and pings Neil in Slack that he should follow up within the next

---

* I held an "Ask Me Anything" or AMA on my book *Slack For Dummies*.

† Cygnus is a fictional composite of ten real companies using internal collaboration hubs that I discovered researching this book.

24 hours. Customers who purchase Cygnus's widgets occasionally call the company's 1-800 number or fill out forms on its website. In either event, Cygnus's employees easily track these tickets in Zendesk. Again, because the company installed the Zendesk app for Slack, notifications take place immediately. No one needs to manually send messages.

I could keep going, but you get my drift. In this example, Slack serves as Cygnus's internal collaboration hub. Continuing with my example, Zendesk, Salesforce, and Google Workspace represent several essential spokes that connect to its collaboration hub.

A hub can—nay, *should*—represent the default mode of internal communication and collaboration for all formal and informal groups.

What do hubs and spokes mean for communication, collaboration, and the future of work?

A lot.

First, compared to email, hubs provide a superior medium for internal communications. People who faithfully use collaboration hubs minimize misunderstandings. Second, they make it easier than ever for colleagues, partners, and vendors to effectively collaborate on documents, files, and projects, no matter where and when they happen to be working.

Three Ways to Connect Spokes to Your Hub

Say that you buy into the Hub-Spoke Model of Collaboration in Figure 6.1. Great, but how does the magic actually happen? Specifically, consider the following pragmatic questions:

- What tools are available to connect spokes to hubs?
- Is a great deal of technical expertise required?

It's time to talk about connective tissue.

Use a Vendor's Native Building Blocks and Connectors

Today's powerful collaboration hubs ship with an impressive array of features, including oodles of out-of-the-box automations and integrations. Put differently, as powerful as Slack, Microsoft Teams, and Zoom are on their own, it's easy to juice up them up even more. I'll focus here on Teams, but you can accomplish similar—if not identical—tasks with the other hubs covered in this book.

A complementary Microsoft tool lets non-technical employees easily create new automations and customize them based upon their individual needs. By using Microsoft Power Automate,* users can build automated workflows† with a few mouse clicks and keyboard taps. Alternatively, they can quickly install an existing workflow template that someone else already published.

---

* Previously known as *Microsoft Flow*.
† I'm not a fan of the term *workflow*, but Microsoft uses it to describe its product.

For example, let's say that you receive weekly project-related updates via email. The emails are a mild annoyance; a private Microsoft Teams channel is the better home for these types of messages.

Yes, you could copy and paste that content into the channel every week, but why bother? Just install the following template:

FIGURE 6.3: Power Automate Template to Post Email to Microsoft Teams

For their part, Slack's proper customers can use Workflow Builder*, a simple, no-code, and increasingly powerful way to streamline and automate manual tasks.[3] For example, automatically welcome a new employee to a public Slack channel or send data to a Google Sheet.[4] Expect the other vendors referenced in Chapter 5 to add similar functionality if they haven't already. It's only a matter of time.

_____

* It's not available under the Free plan.

Use Third-Party Apps

A powerful tool called *If This Then That* connects more than 600 different Web services in useful and often downright innovative ways. As one of millions of examples, IFTTT *applets* let users receive customized weather alerts on their phones.[5]

More apropos to this book, however, IFTTT applets allow for extensive work-related automation. For example, if you want to automatically post a message in Slack when you add a new record to a Google Sheet, have at it.[6] Best of all, IFTTT requires no technical skill. Zilch. With a few clicks, users can just activate existing applets and even create their own.[7]

Airtable, Workato, Formscape, and Zapier function in similar and equally useful manners. Everyday users can automate a wide array of manual tasks. In the process, they facilitate collaboration in unexpected ways. (Chapter 10 delves deeper into this subject.)

In the context of the Hub-Spoke Model, Airtable, IFTTT, Workato, and Zapier allow users to do two critical things:

- Create new integrations between apps and hubs themselves without involving techies.
- Connect spokes, even outside of collaboration hubs.

At a bare minimum, these activities minimize manual work and reduce the chance that someone will forget to alert a colleague of a key task. More broadly, they help accomplish the larger goal of facilitating internal communication and collaboration.

**Non-techies can easily unleash the full
power of today's collaboration hubs.**

Create Custom Bridges

Say that a particularly valuable hub-spoke integration doesn't exist. So much for automation and better collaboration, right?

Not necessarily.

IT departments and developers can use vendors' APIs, SDKs, and webhooks to build custom bridges. (See Chapter 5 for more detail on this topic.) I'm talking about automations, notifications, triggers, and other high-tech means that enable effective collaboration.

Disclaimers

I don't want to overstate things and imply that it's simple to link *every* spoke to a collaboration hub. For two reasons, nothing could be further from the truth.

First, some organizations continue to use legacy applications, systems, and databases. All else being equal, older tech does not play nicely with internal collaboration hubs. Second, not all organizations are created equal. The business needs, regulations, and personnel of a local hospital don't exactly jibe with those of an international retail outfit.

Bottom line: In some cases, the squeeze required to link hubs to individual spokes may not justify the juice.

Getting the Most out of Your Hub and Spokes

The companies maximizing the value from their internal collaboration hubs are linking as many spokes to them as possible. Now that you understand the general framework, how do you get going?

No book of any reasonable length could possibly provide a comprehensive list of all of the ways to collaborate with any single application—let alone all of them. Even if an author somehow pulled off that gangster move, software vendors constantly release new features—and improve existing ones. Such a book would be dated before it hit the shelves.

Fortunately, the Web is replete with valuable resources on all of the hubs and spokes described in this book. Used wisely, they allow you and your colleagues to collaborate better. At a high level, these resources fall into two buckets: official and unofficial.

Official Resources

- Company-run conferences.
- Webinars.
- Feature-specific training videos.
- Websites, blogs, support sites, and forums.
- Private workspaces*

_____

* I'm a proud member of—and contributor to—a number of Slack-run private workspaces. As such, I can pick the brains of hundreds of smart cookies who use Slack in different ways than I do.

Unofficial Resources

- Support forums such as Reddit, StackExchange, and Quora.
- Courses from independent experts on Udemy, Coursera, or LinkedIn Learning.
- Blog posts, YouTube videos, and books from knowledgeable practitioners.
- In-person user groups and Meetups.

There's no shortage of ways to learn how to put your organization's collaboration hubs on steroids—and to avoid the mistakes that others have made.

Collaborating Within and Across Spokes

Many organizations have—knowingly or not—embraced at least some of the Hub-Spoke Model. As a result, their employees excel at collaboration. For reasons that will become apparent in Part III, however, it's possible that hub adoption won't go smoothly. Maybe leadership has committed to deploying Teams or Slack in six months, and you just don't want to wait that long.

Fortunately, you're in luck. The spokes detailed in Chapter 5 ship with some basic collaboration features—and have for years. I'm talking about straightforward ways for employees to work together *within specific software applications*. In these cases, automatic in-app notifications often take the place of having to manually send emails.

Examples

Over the past decade, software vendors have increasingly built in-app collaboration features into their wares. Sadly, relatively few people know about—let alone use—them. I'll bet that you recognize the following scenario.

You use Google Sheets to track a list of customer leads. (You really should be using a proper CRM application such as Salesforce for this purpose, but I digress.) It takes all of two seconds to grant a colleague view, edit, or comment access to that spreadsheet.

Concerned about a colleague mucking up your pristine dataset? Fear not. By default, apps in Google Workspace allow you to easily see changes that others have made—and revert to prior versions if need be.

Here are several simple yet powerful examples of how to use an application's native collaboration features.

Todoist

Consider Todoist, my favorite individual productivity- and task-management application. No one should ever confuse it with proper project-management tools à la Trello, Basecamp, Smartsheet, Wrike, or Asana. Apples and oranges. Still, Todoist allows for some degree of collaboration: Users can delegate tasks to teammates. In-app notifications supplant emails.

Figma and Canva

Professional designers are especially fond of Figma, a web-based tool for collaborative prototyping. Take away its robust collaboration features, and Figma's utility wanes.

By contrast, many amateur designers—and I put myself firmly in this camp—use the graphics-creation tool Canva. Think of it as a lightweight version of Photoshop. Does using Canva, though, mean that I can't collaborate with others?

Hardly.

In no time, I can invite others to view my designs, offer feedback, and even make tweaks.

Spotify (Yes, Spotify)

Unless you work for the company or publish your music or podcasts on it, it's hard to call Spotify a work-related tool. Still, users of the streaming service can create collaborative playlists and let others add songs to them.

Just make sure that you trust them, though: You probably don't want to hear Lady Gaga's latest hit on your "Soft Rock of the 1970s" playlist.

The trend is unmistakable: Software vendors are building more and more collaborative features into their products. Why not take advantage of them?

Benefits

Using spokes to collaborate confers a number of invaluable benefits, including:

- Minimizing the chances of different people creating duplicate versions of the same file—or working with older versions of key documents.
- Reducing the time needed for rework and merging changes from disparate versions of the same document.
- Increasing data quality and integrity.

- Reducing time spent in your inbox.
- Signaling to colleagues that you're not living in 1997. Collaboration today should not entail sending emails and attachments back and forth.

Make no mistake: The advantages of in-app or spoke-based collaboration aren't just theoretical. Rumor has it that Amazon takes draconian measures to prevent employees from generating multiple versions of the same datasets. I have it on good authority that management at The Everything Store[*] has fired people who have sent spreadsheets as standalone email attachments for the very reasons mentioned above.

Limitations

Plenty of folks resist changing how they work—by themselves and with others. Expecting them to willingly move to an internal collaboration hub is a bridge too far. Instead, they opt for half measures in the form of in-app collaboration.

Is this conservative approach better than "collaborating" only via email? Sure, but it doesn't offer the full benefits of using proper collaboration hubs. Although the spokes mentioned in Chapter 5 ship with some handy collaboration features, they don't exist for the primary purpose of getting people to effectively communicate and work together. That's the hub's job.

---

[*] This is the title of Brad Stone's seminal book on the company.

Chapter Summary

- Different activities, goals, and situations require different tools. There is no magical application or technology that handles every conceivable work-related task or function and there never will be.
- Think of Slack, Zoom, Microsoft Teams, and their ilk as internal collaboration hubs. All other applications and systems are spokes in those hubs.
- Collaboration hubs and spokes allow us to automate many routine tasks with zero coding required.

Chapter 7

How to Select an Internal Collaboration Hub

> "Learning to choose is hard. Learning to choose well is harder. And learning to choose well in a world of unlimited possibilities is harder still, perhaps too hard."
> —BARRY SCHWARTZ

The introduction of a proper collaboration hub within an organization is kind of a big deal. (Cue *Anchorman* reference.) In fact, it can represent a major turning point in a company's evolution. In many instances, it's no understatement to call it a *step change*, especially given the extent to which so many companies, departments, groups, and individuals have historically relied upon email.

This chapter reviews the essential questions and considerations when choosing an internal collaboration hub.

Ask the Fundamental Questions

Before you invest too much time in teaching yourself a new tool, start by asking some key big-picture queries.

What Specific Business Problem(s) Does This Software Application Attempt to Solve?

Some newfangled tools fall under the umbrella of *solutionism*: software in search of a problem. If you can't identify the problem(s) that a new application solves, you may want to stop right here.

What Business Problem (s) Does This Application *Not* Solve?

This question is just as important as the previous one. Say that your colleagues generally find Microsoft OneDrive clunky for sharing files and resist using it. Introducing the popular project-management application Asana won't address that issue, even though it certainly lets users attach files to individual tasks.

Do Your Colleagues Already Use a Similar Tool?

Say that you work for a 2,500-person consumer-products company that uses Microsoft Teams as its hub. You are very happy in your current position. Slack certainly solves similar problems, but is it wise to devote a great deal of time to learning it?[*]

---

[*] If management is thinking of permanently moving to Slack, however, that's another matter.

If So, Then How Does the New Tool Compare to the Incumbent?

Is it appreciably better or less expensive? Are your peers likely to find it more user-friendly?

Generally speaking, it's tough to convince others to change if a new tchotchke is ten percent better or more user-friendly than the incumbent. Ditto if it's only marginally less expensive or user-friendly.

Is the Juice Worth the Squeeze?

Ultimately, this is a judgment call. Chapter 3 covers the manifold benefits of adopting internal collaboration hubs. Chapter 10, however, explains the reasons that they may disappoint or fail. An organization that has failed twice before to roll out a new hub may wait before trying again.

Is Now a Good Time?

There may never be a perfect time to adopt the Hub-Spoke Model, but here's one final reason to look before you leap. Companies experiencing massive layoffs, undergoing a restructuring, or merging with another might want to wait until the dust has settled.

Opt for action. Deploy internal collaboration hubs as soon as possible. Don't wait for the "perfect" time.

Can Our Company Use Multiple Collaboration Hubs?

It's a fair question. After all, it's not 1995.

Back then, acquiring new enterprise tech involved laboriously vetting vendors, year-plus sales cycles, drawn-out contract negotiations, complicated installations, centralized IT departments, and extended implementation timelines.

We're living in a vastly different world.

Over the last two decades, workplace technology has concurrently become more democratic, arguably more chaotic, and exponentially quicker to deploy.

For three reasons, the answer to this query is "*Yes.*"

The Rise of Cloud Computing, SaaS, and Freemium

Two popular business models based upon cloud computing make it easy for entire departments, groups, and individuals to use whatever software they like, whether a CIO approves or not.

As I discussed in Chapter 5, the prevalence of software-as-a-service (SaaS) makes using new applications markedly more affordable compared to years past. In a related vein, many vendors (including Slack and Zoom) embrace the *freemium* business model. Using basic functionality costs nothing. Those who want to use enhanced features have to pay for the privilege.

Shadow IT

Plenty of people become frustrated with their organizations' antiquated systems and applications. I've been there myself many times. Two decades ago, there wasn't a whole lot that rank-and-file employees could do about it.

Not anymore.

For years, plenty of departments and groups have circumvented their IT departments and purchased whatever software they wanted. While often understandable, Shadow IT can introduce significant security, compliance, and privacy risks into an organization.

BYOD

For more than a decade, we have been bringing our own devices and applications to the office. Again, this genie is out of the bottle. To state the obvious, remote work makes it even more difficult for IT folks to stop employees from using prohibited devices and apps.

As a result of these three trends, many organizations unknowingly use *tools* (plural) with considerably overlapping or even identical functionality. For example, a large retailer pays several cloud-computing providers, including Amazon, Microsoft, and Google. The company would lower its total tech costs by picking just one of them.

As you might expect, the same principle holds true with other types of software, including collaboration hubs.

The Prevalence of Multiple Collaboration Hubs

Mio sells software that connects Slack, Microsoft Teams, and Cisco Webex Teams. In June 2019, the company published the results of a survey of 200 tech decision-makers.[1]

Its findings shouldn't shock anyone familiar with today's relatively decentralized world of enterprise IT.

In two-thirds of the organizations surveyed, *employees used both Slack and Microsoft Teams*. A common example: Company X relies primarily upon Microsoft Teams but acquires Company Y—a smaller one that had embraced Slack.

An organization *can* select, deploy, and use as many collaboration hubs as it likes. The Slack police won't visit because a rogue department at your firm started using Microsoft Teams or Zoom.

There's a chasm, however, between *can* and *should*.

Collaboration Hubs and Economics 101

> *Your scientists were so preoccupied with whether or not they could they didn't stop to think if they should.*
> —JEFF GOLDBLUM AS DR. IAN MALCOLM, *Jurassic Park*

Let's modify the question from the previous section: Should our company use multiple collaboration hubs?

In a word, *No*. Here's why.

Say that you're stuck in the desert for a few days without any water. Finally, someone rescues you and takes you to a convenience store.

You are dehydrated and buy a 12-pack of bottled water. You pound the first one, crack the second, and repeat. Each successive gulp provides less utility than the first. In fact, drinking too much water can make you sick or, in extreme cases, kill you.[2]

Economists call this phenomenon *the law of diminishing returns*, and it applies to internal collaboration hubs as well.

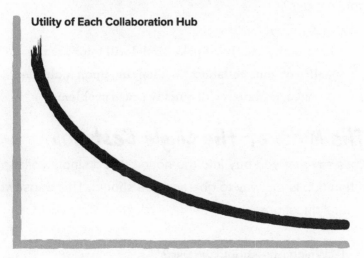

Collaboration Hubs and Diminishing Marginal Returns

Utility of Each Collaboration Hub

Number of Collaboration Hubs Used

FIGURE 7.1: Collaboration Hubs and Diminishing Marginal Returns

Splitting internal collaboration and communication into multiple hubs serves only to:

- Unnecessarily complicate matters.
- Reduce the power and utility of each hub.
- Confuse people.

- Bifurcate knowledge.
- Arguably increase costs.
- Signal to employees that they can do whatever they want.

In short, when it comes to hubs, it's best to pick a lane and stay in it as much as possible. Ditto for spokes for that matter. Why use four different project-management applications?

Embracing the Hub-Spoke Model will improve the quality of your collaboration. Relying upon multiple hubs, however, will quickly cause problems.

The Myth of the Single Best Hub

Let's say that you buy into the notion that a single collaboration hub is the way to go—and you should. This begs two natural questions:

1. Which one should we use?
2. Which is the best collaboration hub?

I'll answer the second question first.

In some cases, a particular hub may offer objectively more powerful bells and whistles than its competition—at least in the short term. Let's say that an über-useful feature distinguishes Slack or Zoom today. As the following sidebar illustrates, though, odds are that Microsoft, Google, and Facebook will quickly mimic it.

> ## Great Artists ~~Steal~~ *Borrow*
>
> Software vendors frequently "borrow" features from one another. Here are a few particularly relevant examples.
>
> For years, Slack users relied upon private channels to hold exclusive group discussions and share files within a workspace. In a glaring omission, Microsoft Teams did not offer comparable functionality. Finally, in late 2019, Microsoft added the very same feature and didn't even bother renaming it.
>
> I use Zoom every day, and not just for video calls. A few months ago, I created an event in Google Calendar and accidentally enabled Google Meet for it. (It's a common mistake. Google has been pushing Meet ever since Zoom exploded in popularity.) After my meeting started and Google Meet launched, I saw that I could easily enable breakout rooms—one of Zoom's signature features.

All software vendors pay close attention to what their competitors are doing. This won't change anytime soon. Over time, their differences will blur even more.

Given that, what are the main factors that an organization should consider when selecting its internal collaboration hub?

Critical Factors

While not a comprehensive list, here are the most prevalent considerations.

Cost and Existing Vendor Relationships

It's downright naïve to pretend that money doesn't matter in any circumstance, let alone during a pandemic and recession.

As I mentioned in Chapter 5, Microsoft bundles Teams with its ubiquitous Office 365 suite. Bottom line: Your organization may already be able to access a powerful collaboration hub at no additional cost. Ditto if your company currently pays for Webex or Google Workspace. These ancillary tools effectively ride for free.

Now consider the other end of the spectrum. To realize the *full* benefits of the same collaboration hubs, you'll have to pay. I'm talking about Slack, Zoom, Teams, and others.

At least there's some good news: These companies charge per user per month. As such, firms don't have to pony up beaucoup bucks to get going. If you want to purchase only ten employee licenses, have at it. Large organizations can pay less per user by opting for all-you-can-eat enterprise plans. Past a certain point, the marginal cost of adding an additional user is zero. Think Vegas buffet.

Say that you want to get a little bit pregnant. It takes all of about five minutes to start kicking the tires of Slack, Zoom, and other collaboration hubs that operate under the freemium model. Just understand, however, that you won't be able to use all of their functionality unless you upgrade from *user* to proper *customer.*

Integrations With Existing Applications

As covered in Chapter 6, collaboration hubs don't—*or at least shouldn't*—exist in a vacuum. An organization or group that uses Slack or Microsoft Teams as a standalone tool realizes only a fraction of its benefits.

To this end, it's time to discuss third-party apps. For example, when I join a new Slack workspace, I always install the Slack app for Zoom in it.[3] That way, I can make and receive Zoom calls *without leaving Slack*. (I then install a number of other apps, but I'll keep it simple here.)

At a high level, collaboration hubs' third-party apps perform a number of valuable functions:

- They enhance or extend the collaboration hub's native functionality.
- They connect the collaboration hub to spokes.
- They automate manual tasks.
- They save employees a significant amount of time.

Cards on the table: For my money, Slack's developer community is hands down the most robust. These talented folks have created thousands of innovative and useful ways to supercharge Slack. More arrive every day. Examples include polls, calendar and time-tracking integrations, productivity and project management tools, networking and social apps, and many more.

Expect Zoom, Microsoft, and the other vendors to catch up here. For now, however, if your organization prioritizes access to the widest array of third-party apps, then also-rans such as Cisco Webex Teams won't make the cut. In this case, it's easier to justify the cost of paying for additional software. The juice is worth the squeeze.

Compliance and Regulations

Healthcare and financial institutions need to abide by different regulations than colleges and universities do. Ditto for a company based in the United States compared to one headquartered in Europe. What's more, laws change.

Scores of professors, doctors, and bankers use Slack, Zoom, Microsoft Teams, and other popular collaboration hubs. Do a little research before walking down the aisle, though. You don't want to face fines or legal problems because you inadvertently used a tool that violates customer, partner, or employee privacy.

Vendor Size and Stability

Say what you will about Microsoft. I prefer Slack to Teams, but Microsoft and Cisco are far more likely to exist ten years from now than Slack, Discord, or even Zoom for that matter. It's not hard to envision any number of scenarios that result in these multi-billion-dollar companies going kaput. That goes triple for a 15-employee startup that has created a chic collaboration tool. It may disappear next month. Conservative organizations tend to prefer stability with their software vendors and tend to make their decisions accordingly.

Just because a company is small, however, doesn't mean that it will vanish. Basecamp and Todoist are just two examples of small shops that have been around for more than a decade and aren't going anywhere anytime soon.

Security

Don't make the mistake of thinking that any application is impenetrable. Collaboration hubs are no exception to this rule. Hackers are a smart lot. As a result, think of security as an ongoing process, not a discrete outcome.

Companies often approach security in somewhat different ways. For example, if end-to-end encryption is an essential requirement at your organization, then you can eliminate applications that currently fail to offer it.

Company Culture and Employee Flexibility

Some organizations, departments, groups, and individuals are more adept at learning new tools than others. At the risk of overgeneralizing, some tools are easier for people to stomach than others.

Consider two fictitious organizations:

- **ABC:** Its workforce has long rejected learning new technologies and systems.
- **XYZ:** Its workforce prides itself on flexibility and the ability to adapt and use new tools as needed.

With no other information, it doesn't take a rocket surgeon to surmise which organization is more likely to successfully adopt a collaboration hub. To this end, ABC's management should think long and hard about purchasing an enterprise Slack, Workplace from Facebook, or Zoom license. That goes double if it already pays for Office 365 and can effectively use Microsoft Teams for free.

What Color Is Your Field?

I described the relatively decentralized nature of contemporary IT earlier in this chapter. As a result, at large companies, it's more than likely that employees are *already* using one or more collaboration hubs whether management has sanctioned it or not. Put differently, it's instructive to think of your situation in relation to three different types of fields:

Type of Field	Description and Implications for Collaboration Hubs
Green	The organization has not dabbled with an internal collaboration hub. People are generally open to the idea of using one or, at least, aren't strongly opposed to it.
Brown	Some people have previously experienced using a hub. Results are decidedly mixed.
Black	The organization attempted to deploy the hub and failed miserably. Wounds are fresh. As a result, people are skeptical about attempting to go down this road again. Think scorched earth.

TABLE 7.1: The Three Fields of Enterprise Technology Adoption

No, it's not impossible for people working in brown and black fields to successfully deploy collaboration hubs. Still, it's usually an uphill battle. All else being equal, green-field organizations are far more likely to reap the benefits of collaboration hubs than their brown and black counterparts. Know this going in.

Does the Vendor Embrace the Hub-Spoke Model?

As Chapters 5 and 6 manifested, Microsoft, Zoom, Slack, and others are embracing the Hub-Spoke Model. Still, not every software vendor does. Some may resist and opt to create walled gardens that make integrating spokes difficult.

Run from these vendors.

It's only a matter of time before they perish. At that point, you'll have to adopt a new internal collaboration hub, train people on how to use it, and deal with all other sorts of change-management issues.

> **Expect software vendors that cling to walled gardens to die on the vine.**

Switching Hubs

What happens if an organization wants to change vendors? Can they port over their essential messages, files, and knowledge from the old hub to the new one?

In short, no magic switch exists to magically transfer over all data and metadata from Microsoft Teams to Slack—or vice versa. This is very much by design: Software vendors generally don't want to make it easy for their clients to take their business across the street.

That's not to say that IT departments, developers, and consultants can't extract public information from Hub A, noodle with it, and eventually import it into Hub B.* After all, we put a man on the moon more than 50 years ago. It's certainly possible, as long as management's desire and budget are up to snuff. More than likely, though, at least some key information won't survive the transition.

> **Select your hub judiciously. Switching to a**
> **new one will not be as easy as you think.**

Collaboration With External Organizations

Up until now, I've focused on the communication and collaboration that take place *within an organization*. I've done this for the sake of simplicity. I'm not oblivious, though: Plenty of interactions occur with non-employees: partners, job applicants, vendors, temps, independent contractors, consultants, and other service providers.

Inviting others to an internal collaboration hub typically takes one of two forms:

1. **Short-term collaboration:** For example, a company is holding its annual conference. Its organizers invite the speakers to join the hub a few months before the event.
2. **Long-term or indefinite collaboration:** This involves establishing a secure, shared channel. For example, two universities' biology departments want to conduct joint experiments for at least the next few years.

---

* Information in private messages and channels, however, will almost certainly remain private.

The first feature is table stakes. All of the major players allow the creation of simple guest accounts. If the second feature is paramount, then Slack is well ahead of the pack as of this writing. Sharing channels via Slack Connect[4] may, in fact, tip the scale in its favor, although other vendors have doubtless added this functionality to their product roadmaps.

Chapter Summary

- If a gangster feature distinguishes Slack or Zoom today, odds are that Microsoft, Google, and/or Facebook will quickly mimic it.
- Among the most important factors that organizations should consider when selecting an internal collaboration hub are cost, security, compliance, company culture, and the need to collaborate with external partners.
- All else being equal, it's easier to deploy a collaboration hub in a green field than in a brown or black one.

Chapter 8

Why Collaboration Hubs Can Disappoint

"Culture eats strategy for breakfast."

—PETER DRUCKER

Chapter 3 listed the manifold benefits that organizations can realize by adopting powerful collaboration hubs. Indeed, they can quickly and dramatically improve how teams communicate and collaborate—especially remotely. Over a long-enough period of time, they can help increase transparency and transform cultures. In Chapter 7, I showed you how to select one.

A + B = C, right?

If only it were that easy.

Enabling collaboration technologies is not all puppy dogs and ice cream. In this vein, Slack, Microsoft Teams, Zoom, and other collaboration hubs share many similarities with other enterprise technologies:

- Sometimes an organization takes a step backward before taking a giant leap forward.
- Internal adoption may not be universal and evenly distributed, especially at large outfits.
- Sometimes the tool fails to take root in the organization altogether.

This chapter describes the most common reasons that collaboration hubs can fail to deliver on their considerable promise.

Employee Resistance to Change

Let's start with the big kahuna: People generally resist changing how they work. Few employees rejoice when management announces that new technologies are coming to the enterprise. By way of background, I've seen this movie many times before. In a word, my first book, *Why New Systems Fail*, is primarily about people.

We often delay making even minor changes—such as upgrading familiar applications. And the results can be devastating. Case in point: On October 7, 2020, Public Health England revealed that nearly 50,000 people exposed to COVID-19 weren't reported. Why? The National Health Service used an outdated version of Microsoft Excel that couldn't accommodate all of the records in a single spreadsheet.[1]

You just can't make this stuff up.

Have you ever suggested to a colleague that there's a better way to accomplish something in Excel or another program? It's possible that your peer thanked you for your tip and started doing things differently. It's just as plausible, however, that you had inadvertently irritated your colleague.

Make no mistake: Hubs face similar challenges. Many folks don't take too kindly to newbies, smarty-pants, or self-proclaimed experts pointing out that they could be working far more efficiently and collaboratively. In this scenario, employees stuck in their ways are unwilling to give the internal collaboration hub a proper chance.

Employee Impatience Begets a Vicious Downward Cycle

Let's say that people are open to using a new collaboration application. A successful outcome is hardly guaranteed for all sorts of reasons.

Back in Chapter 4, I covered why email sucks for collaboration and internal communications. In a nutshell, playing Whac-A-Mole with your inbox isn't a terribly efficient way of working and even increases stress.[2]

Try explaining as much, however, to self-anointed *email ninjas* who believe that they have mastered email over the course of their careers. Spend two hours per day in an application for fifteen or twenty years, and you'll get really good at it, too.

Against that backdrop, remember that learning *any* new software program takes time—including email 20 years ago. The intuitive user interfaces of Slack, Zoom, and Microsoft Teams don't change that immutable law. Email wizards won't *immediately* be as productive as they learn these new tools. In a few weeks, though, the real benefits kick in as long as they give the collaboration hub some time.

Impatient and obstinate people look at things only through short-term lenses. They often become frustrated with collaboration hubs because their productivity suffers. It doesn't take long for them to revert to an old standby: email. If this happens—even at a relatively small scale—then the vicious and inexorable downward cycle begins:

- Fewer people in the organization use the internal collaboration hub.
- Its overall utility wanes.
- The organization's level of internal collaboration suffers.
- This drop causes even fewer people to use the collaboration hub.*

It's a race to the bottom, with predictable results. Best-case scenario: A few groups of employees in the organization use the internal collaboration hub to its fullest capacity. Collaboration is uneven at best.

We're just getting started on why these collaboration hubs don't always bear fruit.

Lack of Sufficient Employee Training

As I explain in Chapter 14, you can teach yourself how to use any collaboration tool if you consistently use it and put the time in. And there lies the rub: It's unreasonable for managers to expect busy employees to teach themselves the ins and outs of using Slack, Microsoft Teams, or Zoom in their spare time.

---

* For this very reason, people are fond of misplacing blame. It's the fault of the software vendors for building a mediocre product.

Companies that provide dedicated, real-time training classes accomplish three key objectives. First, employees' jobs during that time involves learning, not performing their normal daily tasks.

Next, a proper training class—virtual or in-person— provides a dedicated environment in which employees learn how to best use an application. Attendees can ask professionals detailed and job-specific questions. They start to conceptualize how their jobs will change—both for themselves and with others. The new application becomes less abstract to them. As a result, they are more likely to actually use it after class ends.

Finally—and just as important—leadership sends a strong signal to its workforce that using the new internal collaboration hubs is essential.

Unfortunately, many firms skimp on proper training. People rightly infer that using the new hub is optional. If it were really important, wouldn't the company hire an expert to show them how to use it properly?

Lack of Commitment From Senior Leadership

A dearth of proper training is but a symptom of a disease. Senior leadership isn't committed to using the hub. An example will explain what I mean.

To a person, executives at Company X decry its current state of internal communication and collaboration. Teams often work at cross-purposes, resulting in product delays and general confusion. Sound familiar?

The bigwigs at Company X (correctly) believe that a new collaboration tool can help alleviate these concerns. As an existing Microsoft shop, they encourage all employees to rely upon Teams. However, they themselves flout using it.

In its stead, the head honchos hypocritically continue to discuss key issues and make decisions using—wait for it— Outlook. Underlings get sucked into interminable email threads because the Chief Marketing Officer doesn't "do" Teams. No one wants to miss senior-level communications. FOMO at its finest. Eventually, all employees cease using Teams.

Employee Security and Privacy Concerns Result in Limited Usage

I belong to plenty of Slack workspaces. In the past year, I have given a handful of webinars on my favorite collaboration hub. Based on these experiences, one of newbies' most common questions concerns privacy and security: People are sometimes skittish about using Slack because they fear that someone is watching.[*] They feel more comfortable sending sensitive messages to colleagues via the more familiar email.

In terms of security and privacy, there's no appreciable difference between email and collaboration hubs. In either case, your employer owns the tool.[†] In the United States, courts have routinely ruled that employees have no expectation of privacy while using their employers' communication technologies. As Sarah Krouse explained in a July 2019 piece

---

[*] Some have asked me the same question about Zoom.

[†] The only exception is if you're using a free or personal version of the product; that is, your employer isn't footing the bill.

for *The Wall Street Journal*, many people think that their work messages are private. In point of fact, nothing could be further from the truth.[3]

Beyond privacy, many people inherently trust email over new collaboration hubs for one simple reason: familiarity. As a result, they use the former far more than the latter.

This is unfortunate. Mainstream collaboration hubs ship with powerful encryption baked in. It's absurd to claim that email is a fundamentally more secure communications medium than Slack, Zoom, or a similar product. In fact, the latter are more secure because they lock uninvited guests out of them.[*]

Potentially Higher Technology Costs

In Chapter 5, I outlined the SaaS business model. Compared to the old method of purchasing enterprise software and hosting it on-premise, SaaS is far less expensive. However, in a perverse way, renting applications can discourage wide-spread adoption throughout a company.

Consider Slack. As of this writing, its premium Plus plan costs $15 per month, with a modest discount for annual purchases. That means $150 per year per employee to use the tool. In my view, it's money well spent: Eight cents per employee per hour based upon a 2,000-hour workweek to realize its considerable benefits

Still, it's not hard to envision a bean counter asking if *every* department and employee needs access to Slack. For

------

[*] For example, Slack Connect eliminates phishing and spam.

example, a company could refuse to grant Slack licenses to 30 "non-essential" employees to save $4,500 per year.

Again, a collaboration hub works best when everyone in an organization faithfully uses it. Only then can the firm maximize the hub's utility—and the extent to which employees collaborate.

The Organization Screws Up the Implementation

I'll return to this important topic in Chapter 10. For now, suffice it to say that leadership adopts the wrong implementation approach.

When Ego and Organizational Politics Collide

What benefits the organization as a whole may temporarily disrupt one department—and vice versa. Particularly in large, mature, and successful companies, valuable new technologies and initiatives are frequently no match for massive egos and internal politics.

With respect to collaborative tools, let's say that a powerful fifty-something VP (Jeff) built a homegrown application twenty years ago. It's his baby. For a while now, it's been long in the tooth. Employees have been rumbling and starting to use their own tools, much to the CIO's chagrin.

Enter Martha, a brash new executive with grand plans to transform the organization. In her prior role, she successfully deployed a collaboration hub to great fanfare.

It takes all of about five minutes for Martha and Jeff to clash. One represents the new guard while the other is trying to preserve his legacy and hold on until retirement.

Chapter Summary

- Success with any new enterprise technology is hardly a given. Internal collaboration hubs are no exception to this rule.
- With rare exception, collaboration hubs disappoint or fail because of people-related issues, not from any deficiencies in the underlying technologies or applications themselves.
- Holding formal training classes signals to employees that the collaboration hub is an essential workplace tool. If leadership takes it seriously, then everyone else is more likely to do the same.

Part III

Moving From Theory to Practice

chapter 4

Reviewing Implementation Strategies

> *"Change has its enemies."*
> —ROBERT KENNEDY

A swath of new tools makes it easier than ever to work together. Part II of this book provided the requisite framework for a new and better way to collaborate. A hub works best when as many employees as possible in an organization use it.

But where to begin? In other words, how does an organization make that happen?

This chapter provides three different high-level adoption approaches for making the Hub-Spoke Model a reality. Note that the three are not mutually exclusive—especially at large organizations. It's not hard to imagine a firm concurrently employing two of these methods in different pockets.

Bottom-Up

Entry-level employees in an organization organically start using the hub—maybe even under the radar. They may or not be tech-savvy. Regardless of their backgrounds, they are tired of dealing with their overflowing inboxes. They see the individual benefits of connecting hubs and spokes, discussed in Chapter 3. It never occurs to them to ask permission. The powers-that-be either don't notice that employees are using the hub or take a decidedly *laissez faire* approach to IT management.

Although impossible 20 years ago, I have seen this movie before plenty of times at large companies. Employees use an application, system, or other technology without their leadership's knowledge, let alone consent. (See the discussions on BYOD and Shadow IT in Chapter 7.)

Advantages

This decentralized approach generally offers the following advantages:

- **Realizing benefits faster:** By not waiting for leadership to make a firm-wide decision, employees immediately begin accruing the benefits of hubs and spokes.
- **Increasing employee buy-in:** People generally use the hub well because they chose it themselves; no one chose it for them. (There's no resentment or feeling of paternalism.) As such, expect people to get a great deal of mileage out of it.

●—● **Reimagining business processes:** Freed from the shackles of senior management and formal IT-change requests, people connect spokes to hubs in innovative ways that would benefit other pockets of the organization. Employees streamline manual processes in ways similar to those that I describe in Chapter 10.

Disadvantages

Of course, there's no such thing as a free lunch. The downsides of this approach include:

●—● **Increased risks:** Organizations that allow employees to use whatever tool they want may expose everyone to considerable security or privacy risks. Who's to say that everyone in the organization is using the most updated version of the hub's software?

●—● **Potentially higher tech costs:** If four groups each pay separate license fees, total tech costs will likely be higher than if the organization had consolidated its purchases. As any grizzled IT vet will tell you, lack of coordination can be expensive.

●—● **Data silos:** Multiple hubs mean that key data exists in tools that others cannot access. Fusing hubs while preserving all data and metadata is time-consuming and often impossible.

Top-Down

The IT or HR department (or both) thoroughly review their available options. Perhaps they solicit formal requests for information (RFIs) and proposals (RFPs).* A year or more later, they pick a winner. Prolonged contract negotiations ensue. If the company chooses Workplace from Facebook, for example, then it attempts to ensure that employees aren't using the competing hubs from Cisco, Zoom, or Slack.

Advantages

The upsides of this admittedly bureaucratic approach include:

- **A single knowledge repository:** All organizational data and knowledge exist in a single, searchable place.
- **Potentially lower tech costs:** You're better off writing a single monthly check to one vendor than to four.
- **Minimal employee confusion:** People know what leadership has decided. To be fair, though, some of them will not like the outcome.

Disadvantages

Here are the biggest drawbacks of the top-down approach:

- **Time:** Conducting a formal and lengthy vendor-selection process means that employees have to wait months to use the approved hub. As I'm fond of saying, the costs of inaction may exceed the costs of action.
- **Employee resentment:** Some people will resent being forced to use the new hub, especially if they deem it

---

* Most government agencies are required to follow these steps before purchasing any software.

inferior to its predecessor. Invariably, employees find reasons to complain about the new hub. Banning the old one is likely to exacerbate employee disaffection.

● ━ ● **Lost data and knowledge:** Again, porting over information from the prior hub to the new one won't be seamless or comprehensive.

Additional Considerations

Even within the top-down approach, one size doesn't fit all. An organization can opt to deploy the hub in an egalitarian, "big bang" method: All employees can immediately use it. Great, but will they inundate the help desk with calls? Will a bunch of people make costly mistakes because they just don't know any better?

Alternatively, a firm can opt for a more conservative, phased approach. Tackling one department, division, or location at a time allows the organization to learn valuable lessons along the way—and apply them. It can refine plans, make tweaks, and avoid repeating previous mistakes. On the other hand, some employees will become impatient that leadership has put them at the back of the line. They may begin using other hubs in the interim.

Middle-Out

This approach is the equivalent of getting a little bit pregnant. That is, employees wedged somewhere between entry-level and the corner office adopt the internal collaboration hub.

Hub adoption grows laterally. It moves to other groups or departments. Eventually, the hub starts making its way up and down the org chart. Typically, certain departments and employees use the tool more quickly than others. Folks in the HR and legal departments tend to join the party at the end, if at all.

Advantages

The middle-out approach offers the following benefits:

- **See quicker adoption:** Compared to the top-down approach, the internal collaboration hub is more likely to take root in more progressive pockets of the organization.
- **Reveal collaborative employees:** Because use of the hubs is quasi-sanctioned, the organization can identify employees who may resist change. (Chapter 11 explores this topic in more depth.)

Disadvantages

This approach suffers from these disadvantages:

- **Uneven adoption:** Certain employees, groups, and departments will adopt the tool faster than others. Those who haven't yet used the hub may resist it. As such, communication and collaboration on cross-functional teams may suffer.
- **Conflicted employees:** Is using the hub important or not? Employees may justifiably wonder if the organization is really committed to the new hub, collaboration, and change in general.

Waterfall vs. Agile

At a very high level, organizations can launch internal or external products in two diametrically opposed ways:

- **Waterfall or Phased-Gate Method:** An organization rolls out a new tool in a rigid, sequential, or phased manner. Months or years of careful and ostensibly scientific planning come to fruition. Consider launching a new life-saving drug or an enterprise-resource planning system. It has to be perfect from day one. Because of all of the interdependencies, midstream changes are nearly impossible to make.
- **Agile methods:** Scrum and its ilk represent the antithesis of the Waterfall Method. Rather than shipping one massive batch at the end of the project, the organization routinely ships smaller ones. There's no conceit of being able to perfectly plan from day one. The team doesn't just tolerate midstream changes; it encourages them.*

Even if your organization opts for the top-down deployment approach described earlier, lean toward the Agile approach. Don't make the mistake of insisting upon excessive documentation, meticulous planning, months of testing, and painful steering-committee meetings. These stalwarts hamper internal communication and collaboration. They signal to employees

---

* Hidebound organizations often try to split the baby through the horribly named moniker *Agilefall*. They're then surprised when their projects fail.

that management isn't reimagining anything. The internal collaboration hub is just another traditional IT project.

Beyond that, the Agile model is the better one for a simple reason. The Waterfall Method is predicated on an endpoint or finish line. Agile methods, however, are not. Reimagining collaboration is an ongoing process, not a discrete outcome.

Which Approach Is Best?

At the risk of sounding like the archetypal consultant, the answer depends on myriad factors. The needs, budgets, and employee profiles of a six-person bootstrapped tech startup don't jibe with those of a large healthcare organization. Bankers face far more stringent regulations than restaurants do—and for good reason. As in tennis, every shot is contextual. The same maxim applies here.

Sure, forcing employees to adopt new collaboration technologies can work. Generally speaking, though, "want to" almost always beats "have to." It's typically better to encourage folks to move in a particular direction than to twist their arms.

By the same token, though, the workplace has never been a democracy. In the United States, the Constitution doesn't apply at work. Call your boss an asshole if you like, but don't expect protection under the First Amendment. At-will employment is still the rule, not the exception.

Expenses aside, there are real dangers to letting everyone use whatever tool they want. And if you think that you're going to make everyone happy, think again.

Organizations looking to make the best decision often benefit from the whisperings of an experienced, independent, and tech-savvy advisor. Yeah, consultants often get a bad rap, but they often serve as invaluable sounding boards. (Yes, I count myself as one of them.)

Chapter Summary

- Organizations that want to deploy internal collaboration hubs can opt for one of three approaches: Bottom-up, top-down, and middle-out.
- Each strategy inheres different costs and benefits. There is no single formula for determining which one is best.
- Experienced and tech-savvy change-management consultants can help organizations choose and implement the best tool and approach. In turn, the firm will minimize the hub's downsides and maximize its benefits.

chapter 10

Reimagining Business Processes

*"If you can't describe what you are doing
as a process, you don't know what you're doing."*

—W. EDWARDS DEMING

By now, it should be apparent that a new model, collaborative mindset, and new technologies can pay big dividends, even if you're not terribly tech-savvy. That's a broad statement, and maybe even an obvious one.

Now it's time to show, not tell.

This chapter analyzes several obsolete business processes and redesigns them in a way that maximizes collaboration. As you'll soon learn, the Hub-Spoke Model can radically improve existing business processes. After all, the vast majority of processes are collaborative.

**If technology vastly improves, then why should
existing business processes remain unchanged?**

Employee-Expense Submission, Approval, and Reimbursement

The global pandemic temporarily put the kibosh on work-related travel and expenses. The hospitality, restaurant, travel, and entertainment industries are reeling—and will for years.[1]

Still, at some point during your career, your boss probably asked you to travel for work. As a result, you booked your ticket, boarded a plane, took a Lyft or Uber, stayed at a hotel, and ate a meal or two.

Companies often provide bigwigs with corporate credit cards. In this case, CXOs and VPs aren't paying for these expenses out of their own pockets. Regardless of whether you had to chase down the money, I'm willing to bet that that entire process hasn't always been glitch-free.

Legacy Process

The specific steps vary from firm to firm, but the following process—or a close facsimile—is hardly uncommon:

1. An employee (let's call her Marie) takes a business trip to Belize for her employer, Beneke Fabricators.*
2. When she returns, she downloads a PDF from the company's intranet and dutifully fills out the form.
3. Marie finds the physical copies of all of her receipts.

---

* *Breaking Bad* fans will appreciate the references in this section.

4. She scans them and then attaches them to an email that she sends to her manager, Walt.

5. Walt briefly peruses Marie's expenses and doesn't notice any glaring charges.

6. He forwards Marie's email to Skyler in the finance department. Walt uses the subject "Expenses Approved" in the subject line of the email.

And, suddenly, things break bad.

7. Skyler notices a potential issue: Marie spent $100 at dinner on Tuesday night. The company policy is quite clear: $40 is the maximum allowable limit.

8. Skyler rejects Marie's expense report. She emails Marie explaining her decision, copying Walt as well.

9. Marie receives the email and becomes upset. Before taking the trip, she had mentioned to Walt that she'd be taking a prospect (Hank) out to dinner. Walt agreed with Marie's decision. As such, the $40 limit shouldn't apply.

10. Marie responds to Skyler's email and copies Walt on it.

11. Back and forth they go, over email, over the next four days.

12. Skyler ultimately informs Walt and Marie that she'll have to get her boss, Ted, involved. Unfortunately, he's on vacation for the next two weeks. Ted refuses to check email because he knows that he'll get sucked into all sorts of issues.

13. Marie is displeased. The expenses total nearly $2,000.

14. Ted returns from his vacation and starts digging himself out of email hell.
15. Nearly two weeks later, Ted approves Marie's entire expense report.
16. Accounting notifies payroll to include Marie's full expense reimbursement in the next biweekly check run.
17. Finally, a little more than two months after taking a business trip, Marie finally receives payment for her business expenses.

No, this cumbersome process isn't the norm for expense reimbursement at Beneke. Still, it illustrates the fact that legacy business processes lend themselves to delays, rework, and employee frustration. In short, they are often not very collaborative.

Collaborative, Hub-Spoke Process

If you think that adopting the Hub-Spoke Model could make this process more efficient and more collaborative, trust your instincts. How 'bout something like this?

1. Like all employees at Beneke, Marie uses the Expensify mobile app.
2. She takes pictures and screenshots of all receipts with her smartphone. That way, she doesn't need to hold on to a bunch of physical receipts.
3. When she arrives home, she submits the expense report in Expensify. (No scanning or email necessary.)
4. Beneke intelligently uses Slack as well as Expensify. All employees have also activated the Zapier Expensify

integration with Slack. Because of this, Marie's action *automatically* creates a private direct message (DM) and subsequent notification in Slack for both Walt and Skyler.[2]

5. Walt looks at the expense report and doesn't see any problems. Onward and upward.

6. Skyler notices the same questionable dinner charge. She sees that Marie and Walt are available in Slack by virtue of their green status indicators.

7. Skyler quickly hops on a video call with both of them and shares her screen. (No time wasted searching for documents.) It takes all of about 45 seconds to get to the root issue.

8. Skyler still needs to get Ted's approval, but here's the rub: When he's on vacation, Ted checks Slack for important internal messages every few days. Marie's matter certainly qualifies; Ted doesn't want colleagues such as Marie to sit in administrative limbo.

9. Two weeks later, Marie receives the expense reimbursement in her paycheck.

Boom.

Even when an exception occurs, the Hub-Spoke Model is more likely to yield a quick resolution.

Diagnosing a Technical Issue

We've all had to call the IT help desk at some point about technical issues. Regardless of why, the process is never enjoyable. Still, there are ways to make it far more collaborative, reduce frustration, and resolve the issue faster.

Legacy Process

Again, the exact process varies from place to place, but the following scenario is common. Note that the firm in this example uses Zendesk as its ticket-tracking system.

1. The employee (Lucy) initiates the process by calling an internal phone number or filling out a form on the company intranet. (If it's the latter, then the form generates a ticket in Zendesk as well as an email to Lucy.)
2. A support rep (Steve) picks up the phone or receives the email. (If it's the former, then the rep will manually create the Zendesk ticket.)
3. Lucy receives an auto-response, usually containing the ticket number for future reference.
4. Steve answers the phone and reviews the ticket.
5. Lucy provides essential information about the issue. Examples include the operating system, the version of the program, and the like. Maybe she even includes a few screenshots.
6. Steve researches the issue. He may ask Lucy for additional information—again, often via email.

The asynchronous communication continues. Depending on the complexity of the problem, resolving it may take a day, a week, or more.

Collaborative, Hub-Spoke Process

A more collaborative, synchronous, and overall better process looks like this:

1. Lucy initiates the ticket within *the internal collaboration hub.*
2. Zendesk automatically creates a ticket and sends a notification to the dedicated Slack channel that all support reps can see.[3]
3. Lucy receives an alert in the hub with the ticket number.
4. Steve needs more information to investigate the issue. Instead of sending her a direct message (DM) through the hub, though, he notices her green status. This means that she's available to chat.
5. Lucy uses the hub to share her screen with Steve. He asks her for permission to record the session and to take control of her mouse.[*] She agrees.
6. Steve acquires all of the information that he needs to investigate the problem.

Resolving the issue may still take some doing, but Lucy will have spent a fraction of the time and effort addressing it. As a result, she's much less likely to become frustrated.

Publishing a Book

Even if your interest in writing a book is zero, give this section a read. Odds are that you will be able to identify many inefficient

---

[*] Lucy also could have recorded the issue herself using Zoom, Loom, or any number of other applications.

steps that would benefit from adopting the Hub-Spoke Model. You can then apply these lessons to comparable processes at your own company.

On the front of most books, you'll see a single moniker prominently displayed: that of the author. (*Reimagining Collaboration* is no exception.) Make no mistake, though: plenty of individuals collaborate in bringing a book to market. Depending on the type of book that the author writes and publication method that she employs,* the following individuals can play key roles:

- The author's agent.
- The publisher's acquisition editor (AE)[†].
- The project editor or manager.
- The interior designer, cover designer, and graphics creator[‡].
- The developmental editor.
- The copy editor.
- The proofreader.
- The indexer.
- The e-book-conversion specialist.
- Researchers.
- Fact-checkers.

---

[*] For example, authors who self-publish their books often opt not to hire professional editors, indexers, proofreaders, and the like.

[†] This is the individual who effectively makes the deal with the author and his agent.

[‡] Often one individual wears all three hats.

In point of fact, it's simplistic to think of bringing a book to market as a single process. Rather, it's a series of orderly, related subprocesses, during which time plenty of back-and-forth takes place among the parties involved. (For example, you can't index the book before it is laid out.) Add the time crunch associated with producing a particularly timely book, and the opportunity for error multiplies.

Legacy Process

Before continuing, two notes are in order. First, the following example is a composite based upon dozens of conversations I've had with successful authors who have worked with traditional publishers over the last two decades.

Second, Malcolm Gladwell, Toni Morrison, and other A-list authors will tell far different tales than the one that mid-tier authors do. Their rock-star status affords these folks white-glove treatment from their publishers. (Think first-class or chartered flights.) They sell so many books that they can take their talents wherever they want if their publishers disappoint or frustrate them. The accoutrements afforded to bankable stars and artists in any industry have never been greater.

By contrast, consider authors in the middle of the curve who work with traditional publishers. They don't receive anywhere near the same treatment from their publishers. What's more, this group typically lacks any transparency into the publication process. That is, they cannot view any sort of project plan, nor will they receive any updates to it. At best, an AE will provide a list of key dates in an emailed contract that the author has to print out, sign, scan, and return via email.

In many instances, authors interact only with their AEs. They cannot communicate directly with the others who play key roles throughout the project. Should one of those editors be unavailable or swamped with work, key questions can go unanswered for weeks at a time. On the publisher's side, one key defection can delay a book's publication date by months.

Here's another challenge for the author: AEs at large publishers often manage dozens of concurrent projects.

As you probably have guessed, email is the *lingua franca* throughout the publishing process—even if an author prefers to use a proper collaboration hub. Old-school editors often resist using collaborative tools such as Google Docs to view and comment on outlines, tables of contents, and drafts of chapters. They've been working a certain way for a long time, and they're not about to change their established processes.

Authors may have to ask their AEs four or five times for basic tasks to be completed. Even then, things tend to fall between the cracks, some of them downright astonishing.

For example, I know authors whose publishers have forgotten to proofread their books before they went to print.* As a result, the book shipped with an uncomfortable number of errors, embarrassing both the author and the publisher. Readers notice. They aren't exactly shy about taking authors to task in their Amazon reviews.

Over the years, authors have ranted about their books' poor paper quality, inscrutable figures, and other galling issues that you wouldn't expect from respected publishers.

---

* Such a glaring omission is tantamount to running payroll without calculating taxes and deductions.

A few have confided in me that their publishers could not deliver bulk book orders to conferences prior to their speaking engagements. Oh, and their publishers' marketing budgets for their books were exactly zero.

Quite a few successful scribes eventually reach their breaking points. It's no coincidence that many have broken with traditional publishers once and for all. Hybrid publishers have become viable options for authors who demand more from their partners than mere printing, use of the logo, and the aegis of credibility.*

Collaborative, Hub-Spoke Process

Whether you've ever written a book or not, it's not hard to envision a better, far more collaborative method to publish one. Such a process wouldn't be predicated on email and asynchronous communication. At a high level, the same people are involved, and the same activities ultimately need to take place. However, *the way in which they take place* could not be more different.

Specifically, the individuals involved actually talk to each other from time to time; the author does not need to route every communication through an AE, who then reroutes it to someone else.

And here's where collaboration hubs prove their mettle:

- From the onset, the team selects an internal collaboration hub, such as Slack.

---

* Motion Publishing is such a publisher.

- As for signing a contract, the publisher reinforces the collaborative nature of the process by using the DocuSign Slack app.[4] No email back and forth.
- Formal meetings take place, but the parties use a scheduling tool, such as YouCanBook.me, Calendly, or Doodle. Those spokes connect easily to hubs.
- Informal meetings frequently take place through the hub, typically after one person sends a quick direct message.
- People use the hub to share their screens and minimize confusion. Synchronous communication quickly gets everyone on the same page.
- The publisher relies upon a proper project-management application, such as Asana or Trello. As a result, the author can easily view who's doing what when and provide updates to specific tasks. The level of transparency is remarkable.
- The author creates her figures in Canva and invites the designer to her Canva team. She dutifully views the art and offers suggestions to improve readability.
- The author next starts a Google Doc. The AE and the project editor can view them and enter comments. (No email attachments required.)

Additional Processes

Researching this book, I discovered plenty of other redesigned business processes that effectively follow the Hub-Spoke Model introduced in Chapter 6. It turns out that organizations can make the following activities more automated, collaborative, and efficient:

- Hiring applicants.
- Tracking and disseminating logistics information.
- Approving travel requests.
- Generating and signing contracts via the DocuSign Slack app.[5]

Even better, redesigning these processes doesn't require mad technical skills. In the words of Will Sanders, founder and CEO of Recruiting from Scratch,[6] "The tools available today allow everyday users to connect different apps and streamline their business processes."

Chapter Summary

- Equipped with new tools, a new mindset, and collaborative colleagues, you can dramatically improve inefficient business processes at your company.
- Don't pooh-pooh the importance of transforming simple business processes. Doing so sets an important example—one that others will hopefully follow.
- The older the process, the less likely that it has changed, and the more likely that the Hub-Spoke Model can improve it.

Chapter

Collaboration Killers and How to Handle Them

> *"The real problem is not whether machines think but whether men do."*
>
> —B. F. SKINNER

Anyone who has worked for more than a year realizes that collaboration is far easier in theory than in practice. Effective collaboration requires more than reading about a new model, rolling out a new hub, connecting some spokes, and crossing your fingers. A single fly or two in the soup can be particularly problematic.

In this chapter, I detail seven real-world scenarios in which individuals failed to effectively collaborate with their colleagues.* I also offer some solutions for handling these delicate situations.

---

* Note that I have changed all of the individuals' names in this chapter.

Holdout Henry

Plenty of organizations, departments, and teams embrace internal collaboration hubs, soon see their benefits, and never turn back. Although it may take a while to adjust, most employees prefer using them to email. If anything, they regret having waited so long to move to Slack or Microsoft Teams. Never mistake *most* with *all*, though.

Background

An organization adopted Microsoft Teams. Internal email has all but disappeared. Maybe this book even helped.

There's just one catch.

A senior employee, whom I'll call Henry, is addicted to Outlook. He flat-out refuses to use Teams.

Henry's stubbornness adversely affects others. Conversations become bifurcated. People wonder why Henry is so special. Maybe they don't need to use Teams, either.

Solution: Emphasize the Importance of Using the Hub

Start with carrots: Advise Henry that Teams is easy to learn and will save him time. (Both happen to be true.) He'll receive fewer emails. His messages will benefit from greater context. Yadda, yadda, yadda. . . .

Next up, nudges—a topic that I explore in Chapter 13. People could respond to his emails with "Good point. I'm responding in Teams," or something a little snarkier.*

---

* This technique worked for me with students during my professor days.

If these techniques don't pan out, then bring out the sticks. Maybe it's time to put Henry on a performance-improvement plan. Ultimately, he might want to "pursue other opportunities." Yes, effective collaboration and hubs are that important.

Inefficient Irene

Sometimes people follow a process long after it makes sense.

Background

While at ASU, like many of my colleagues, I would interview external candidates for open professor positions. At the end of the day, the chair of the hiring committee, whom I'll call Irene, would routinely email a Word document as an email attachment to each interviewer to complete.

Yikes.

A web-based survey via Google Forms or Qualtrics would make it far easier for interviewers to submit their evaluations. (Most department professors already used both tools.) Second, it would quickly collate interviewers' ratings for Irene.

Solution: Show, Don't Tell

I wasn't especially chummy with Irene, but we were certainly cordial. I asked her one day if she had ever used online survey tools. She had. I then gently suggested using one of them to aggregate candidate feedback.* Without condescending or mansplaining, I offered to create a simple one for her to send

---

* I follow a similar process when collecting book endorsements. All data winds up in a single Google Sheet.

and tweak. To quote a lyric from a great Rush song, "Show, don't tell."

Unfortunately, Irene ignored my recommendation—and I wasn't about to force the issue. As the old proverb goes, you can lead a horse to water, but you can't make it drink.

Emily the Email Addict

A few exceptions aside, the folks in corner offices spend most of their time in meetings and their inboxes. (For more on this subject, see the discussion on Manager vs. Maker Time in Chapter 2.) As such, they can cluelessly bludgeon others with emails.

Background

At ASU, professors created their own syllabi to distribute to their students at the beginning of each semester.* For obvious reasons, ASU administrators wanted to ensure that all syllabi contained identical language on key university policies.

All organizations update their policies from time to time, and universities are no exception to this rule. During the start of one semester, a senior administrator, whom I'll call Emily, sent three separate emails to more than two hundred faculty members over the course of two days. Each email contained revised information about newly required language on each course syllabus.

Let's say that a single faculty member dutifully incorporated Emily's changes into her different syllabi after receiving each

---

* Some departments have started mandating standardized syllabi. So much for academic freedom.

message. We're talking about six to nine total changes taking about two minutes each. Now multiply that number by 200. Conservatively, we're talking about upwards of 30 hours of faculty time better spent doing other things.*

Solution: Think Different

Emily's colleagues or boss should gently encourage her to cease the email torrents and, to borrow a phrase from Apple, think different.

Specifically, it would be far more efficient for each course syllabus to link to the same university webpage. That way, an administrator with sufficient privileges could effectively alter the standard syllabus language *for everyone*. This new process would ensure consistency and eliminate the need for busy professors to perform these low-value chores.

Junior Julie

Newly hired employees may recognize the fundamental flaws of email. They may even be willing to abandon it for an internal collaboration hub. Whether they can ultimately convince their superiors to adopt the hub, though, is another matter altogether.

Background

A large public utility had relied upon mass emails for the last quarter-century. Julie joined the organization in an

---

* Because Emily didn't specify her changes in each new email, professors who tweaked her clunky wording had to spend a few extra minutes figuring out what was new this time.

administrative role and took her cues from her manager, Carmela. After all, Julie didn't want to start her new job off on the wrong foot. It wasn't long before Julie's emails began flooding everyone's inboxes.

Christopher was an iconoclast. He prided himself on using collaborative tools as much as possible. When he saw what was happening with Julie, he talked to her (in person) and asked if she had heard of Slack. She had and was curious about it. Christopher recommended that she use it in lieu of email. Strangely, her emails kept coming.

It turns out that Julie had asked Carmela about the possibility of using Slack. Carmela opposed it. In a message rife with Orwellian overtones, Julie informed Christopher that email would remain the company's "medium for official organizational communication."

Solution: Respect the Role

Christopher knew that he wouldn't win this battle, and he certainly wasn't going to blame Julie. She was open to using Slack, but Carmela had emphatically slammed that window shut.

At least Christopher had put the bug in Julie's and Carmela's heads. If enough people started clamoring for Slack (admittedly a long shot at a large utility), then perhaps the organization would change its antiquated ways.

Overzealous Oliver

Plenty of people resist using collaborative tools. Some over-eager folks, however, go too far in the other direction.

Background

Generally speaking, healthcare is not the most dynamic of industries. Although nurse turnover is a thorny problem,[1] many employees tend to stick around, and enterprise technology there isn't exactly cutting-edge. Change happens slowly, if at all.

A newly hired mid-level manager named Oliver is full of piss and vinegar. He sees inefficiencies all around and wants to shake things up. In his first week, he sets up an internal collaboration hub. He urges people to use it, despite their apathy, protestations, and lack of formal training.

It doesn't work.

Solution: Play the Long Game

Oliver's heart may be in the right place, but he's pushing too hard, too fast. (Self-awareness isn't his strength.) He hasn't even received his first paycheck, and he's already implicitly telling his new colleagues that their way of working is all wrong. *He* knows best.

It's best for Oliver to take a few steps back. He should first build some credibility in the organization and establish solid relationships with his peers. After he has completed those things, others will be more likely to seriously consider his recommendations.

Michael the Micromanager

For my money, micromanagers are the single most maddening and least collaborative colleagues. Working effectively with control freaks is usually an exercise in futility. They simply cannot accept feedback or do anything differently, never mind truly collaborating with others.

Background

> *"Academic politics are so vicious precisely*
> *because the stakes are so small."*
> —WALLACE SAYRE

At a large midwestern university, different professors teach sections of the same business *survey course* MGMT-201.[*] By design, these types of courses quickly cover a wide variety of concepts. Sophomores effectively sample all of the material that they will learn over the rest of their college careers. As I know from personal experience, given the breadth of topics covered, teaching a survey course is absolutely dizzying.

One semester, Michael, Samir, and Peter taught multiple sections of MGMT-201. Fortunately, Peter was on good terms with the other two. The three of them had even socialized a bit outside of work.

In the parlance of academia, Bill (the chair of the Management Department) appointed Michael to serve as the course coordinator. As such, Michael had to ensure that all students effectively learned the same material—regardless of the section's nominal professor. For example, Samir couldn't skip the marketing material just because he didn't feel like covering it.

---

[*] Marketing, finance, economics, business communication, information technology, and supply chain are all on the menu. Think wide, not deep.

At the beginning of the semester, Michael suggested that the three of them use Slack to communicate and collaborate. Impressed, Peter and Samir had high hopes for working with him. Slack would allow them to easily ask each other questions and suggest improvements to the material, class exercises, and the like.

Boy, were they wrong.

Michael quickly showed his true colors: He was more course *commander* than *coordinator*. As Peter and Samir would soon learn, all of the professors who had previously taught MGMT-201 expressed the same frustrations about working with him.

It was a nightmare—and Slack didn't ameliorate the situation one iota. (Even the Hub-Spoke Model wouldn't have made a difference here.) Some specific examples of Michael's egregious behavior included:

- He occasionally provided the latest decks of his slides to Peter and Samir a few hours before their classes began. As a result, they had very little time to synthesize his changes, prepare for their classes, and effectively teach the material.
- Michael would not let Samir and Peter communicate directly with the MGMT-201 grading assistants. Michael insisted that they route even straightforward questions through him. As a result, it sometimes took days for Peter and Samir to answer their students' simple questions, such as when their assignments would be graded.
- Michael denied the other professors' requests to change course content, no matter how trivial. He

promised to consider them next year, but Peter and Samir suspected that he was just trying to placate them.

- Michael forbade Peter and Sumir from altering a single test or quiz question. They were all identical across all of the sections. If you think that this action maximizes student cheating, trust your judgment.
- At the end of the first semester, Michael suddenly and inexplicably deleted the Slack workspace containing all of the team's correspondence and suggestions.[*]

Michael, Samir, and Peter had had a number of heated discussions about the former's dictatorial style. Peter and Samir found it suffocating and infantilizing. For his part, Michael ardently defended his style. He maintained that he was doing precisely what Bill wanted. "You're mad at the wrong guy," he told them more than once.

That claim was bullshit. Both Peter and Samir had taught courses with other course coordinators, each of whom gave their peers wide latitude to cover the requisite material.

Resolution: No Happy Ending

Unfortunately, this story doesn't end well.

Peter and Samir could have just said the Serenity Prayer or bit their tongues. Maybe Michael would change his ways. Instead, they informed Bill—a complaint that he doubtless had heard about Michael before.

---

[*] Check out "The Coworkers You Hate" on Slack at https://bit.ly/nog-slack-hate.

Peter and Samir knew the department politics. They weren't going to win that battle. Let's just say that they didn't exactly weep when Bill assigned them different courses to teach next semester. Peter started disengaging at work and soon left the university.

With a fresh pair of colleagues, Michael continued his non-collaborative ways. Case in point: Before the next academic year, he unilaterally changed the primary textbook for MGMT-201. Remarkably, a professor learned about the change from one of her students a few days before classes commenced.

What Should Have Happened

Knowing Michael's prior track record, Bill should have sternly laid down the law when things came to a head. Bill should have told him in no uncertain terms that this type of behavior doesn't fly because it fractures the department.

After that, Michael should have sincerely apologized to Peter and Samir and promised to truly collaborate with them in the future. If Michael did not immediately and permanently change his ways, then Bill should have promptly shown him the door.[*]

Barry the Blissfully Unaware Dentist

Often people who collaborate inefficiently are not deliberately trying to get your goat. They honestly don't know that there's a better way to do something.

---

[*] Michael had not earned tenure and was not on the tenure track.

Background

In late 2010, I started building a website for a kindly, sixty-something dentist in Massachusetts, whom I'll call Barry. He had read *The New Small*, my book about how small businesses were increasingly adopting emerging technologies. Barry decided that he should finally enter the Internet Age.

I could tell from the get-go that Barry struggled with technology.* Removing any last shreds of doubt, one morning I awoke to find that he had sent me 59 different emails, each of which included a separate PDF attachment of a client testimonial that he wanted to feature on his new website.

Solution: Go Old School

Calm down. Pick up the phone and call him. Make sure that he's in front of a computer with a high-speed Internet connection so you can share your screen with him. Explain to him that there's a much better way to share files—and walk him through the process. (Zipping individual files or putting them in Dropbox, Google Drive, or Microsoft OneDrive are just a few of them.)

Beyond that, explain that he's not the first person to make this mistake. If he has questions about how to share files or remotely collaborate in general, remind him that you'll be there to help him.

---

* Adding to my sympathy for him, he told me that he had recently shattered his pelvis. Ouch.

Chapter Summary

- Pushing too hard, too fast with new collaboration tools may backfire.
- Some folks will resist adapting to more collaborative methods and tools, even if you ask nicely.
- Micromanagers are generally allergic to collaboration. The Hub-Spoke Model doesn't change that fact at all.

chapter 12

The Myths of Collaboration

"If you know the enemy and know yourself, you need not fear the result of a hundred battles."

—SUN TZU

Singing, public speaking, training, and writing have a great deal in common. Just about anyone *can* do these things. Relatively few people, however, do them *well*.

For example, I fancy myself an effective public speaker, trainer, and writer. If push came to shove, I *could* sing. The idea, however, that any sane person would pay me to belt out a tune is risible.

As a parallel, anyone *can* collaborate, but not everyone does it *effectively*. To overcome that gap, it's essential to understand the difference between the two. The next step involves identifying the myths that inhibit reimagining collaboration.

I've grouped them into the following three buckets:

- General.
- Teams.
- Technology.

Let's rock.

General

Here are some common myths about collaboration.

Collaboration Is Easy

Let's say that you have worked with the same core group of colleagues for the past four years. The five of you can practically finish each other's sentences. It's a little scary. The term *work wife* or *work husband* comes to mind.

Long ago, the team had collectively established formal work rules about vacation time and preferred applications. More important, you all know—*and respect*—the informal norms that have developed over time. You call yourselves *The Dream Team*.

That's not to say that occasional kerfuffles don't occur. In a way, though, these minor disagreements and skirmishes are healthy: the team's levels of trust, commitment, and communication allow for quick and amicable resolution.* No one burns any bridges.

---

* Everyone has read Patrick Lencioni's bestseller *The Five Dysfunctions of a Team: A Leadership Fable.*

Congratulations: Your team is the exception that proves the rule.

Effective collaboration is a tough nut to crack, even if your team uses state-of-the-art tech. If you follow every recommendation in this book, there's still no guarantee that a small team—never mind a large department or entire organization—will work well together.

Collaboration Is Binary

Bullshit. There are degrees. One department, team, or group may collaborate far better than another.

Collaboration Is Static

Along these lines, it's folly to think of collaboration as static. It can change over time for all sorts of reasons. Here are a few:

- A team adds a new member who needs time to get up to snuff.
- A key employee begins experiencing personal problems that make him less collaborative.
- Intra-team tensions eventually come to a head. (Chapter 11 covers a related example.)

Collaboration Means Being on Video Calls All Day

To be sure, at some point you'll listen to—or participate in—a video call. Zoom and its ilk facilitate synchronous communication and collaboration.

Still, the idea that you're collaborating only if you're on a videoconference is patently ridiculous. Nothing could be further from the truth.[1] All else being equal, managers will take more Zoom calls than makers. Still, it's hard to envision many situations in which someone *routinely* spends her entire workday in front of a webcam.

Synchronous and Asynchronous Communication Are Equivalent

Introverts are generally loath to talk to people. As such, they're apt to concur with the following statement: Asynchronous, text-based tools obviate real-time, in-person communication.

Again, that's a myth.

Yes, in certain circumstances, sending someone a quick message or commenting on a shared document eliminates the need for a proper conversation. Still, sometimes it's beneficial or even essential to pick up the phone and/or share your screen with a colleague. (The examples in Chapter 10 manifest the benefits of synchronous communication.)

Long before I began using today's popular collaboration hubs, I advocated following a three-email rule.[2] After three, it's time for one person to call the other.

Reimagining Collaboration Happens Immediately

Say that you want to lose 25 pounds. Absent liposuction, it won't happen overnight. Rather, you'll have to change some of your behaviors—and adopt new ones. Eating less and exercising more are two natural starting points.

Along these lines, you cannot wave a magic wand and make effective collaboration appear. *Presto!*

If only it were that easy.

All Collaboration Is Created Equal

Complex, multi-year projects usually involve hundreds of meetings, thousands of informal conversations, and countless other interactions. Conversely, small-scale collaborations are far simpler. As such, they should be much less prone to conflict and misunderstandings.

I fondly recall dozens of simple, discrete, and seamless interactions I've had with others over the years. In some cases, a new client or vendor and I accomplished a task in 30 minutes that otherwise would have taken hours.

No one bats 1.000 though, including me. It's a mistake to assume that everyone will collaborate well together—*even on simple tasks*. As the following two examples illustrate, gridlock isn't the sole purview of a divided government.

Contributing to a Book

I was talking to an acquaintance of mine (Will) as I was putting the finishing touches on *Zoom For Dummies* in 2020. Serendipitously, we started discussing whether he could contribute a short sidebar. After a few minutes, we agreed that the book would benefit from his perspective—as long as he could produce it quickly.[*]

Collaborating would require a few different tools. First, I quickly created a Google Doc and shared it with him. That way, we could refine his contribution together if needed. Second, my publisher, Wiley,

---

[*] As a fellow independent trainer, I thought that the book might generate some leads for him.

required that all contributors sign a standard legal form. I generated a custom PDF for Will to sign, put it in my Dropbox, and pasted a link to it as a comment in our Google Doc.

A few minutes after receiving these notifications, Will emailed me. His personal collaboration system didn't include mainstream tools such as Google Docs and Dropbox. He certainly wouldn't learn them on my account. If I wanted his contribution in my book, then I would have to play by *his* rules.

Faced with a tight deadline and an already lengthy manuscript, I opted not to argue with Will. *Zoom For Dummies* shipped without his sidebar.

That wasn't the only time that a potential collaborator and I didn't see eye to eye.

When setting up a meeting, emailing available times and days back and forth is so 1998. For years, I've happily used the online scheduling service YouCanBook.me. Tools like it expedite the process of booking meetings. Set up an account and send others your link. They need only to look at your available slots, pick one that works for them, enter a little information, and the calendar invite is on its way. That's it. Mic drop. See for yourself in Figure 12.1.

Unfortunately, everyone eventually encounters a person who considers the very idea of using someone else's time-saving tool to be a personal affront or some sort of perverse power play.

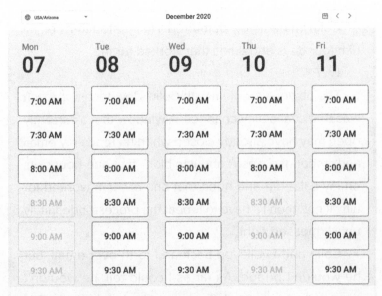

FIGURE 12.1: My YouCanBook.me Page

Getting Off on the Wrong Foot

A while back, I was thinking of developing a training course for a prominent online-learning outfit.

After my agent made the standard virtual introductions, I dutifully sent my contact Colin a link to my scheduling page. I mentioned to him that, if he provided me with a link to a similar scheduling tool, I would gladly use his in lieu of my own.

As was the case with Will, I didn't give it a second thought. Hundreds of people have used my YouCanBook. me link to quickly book time with me over the years—and I'm not even that popular.

Colin immediately demurred. He insisted that I email him four days and times that worked for me.

WTF?

The obvious problem with Colin's low-tech approach was that availability changes. A window that's currently open may have already closed when he reads my email and responds. I wasn't about to block four one-hour slots on my calendar and hope that one of them worked for him. If not, then I'd have to repeat the process indefinitely until I guessed right.*

Colin and I volleyed back and forth over email, but he wouldn't budge. As far as I could tell, he wouldn't even look at my scheduling page. My agent soon called me and told me to chill. I bit my tongue, complied, and emailed him a bunch of available windows.

Colin and I eventually figured out a time to talk. Ultimately, however, we didn't work together. My proposed class just wasn't a fit for his portfolio.

I wasn't heartbroken. Based upon our initial interactions, I suspected that collaborating with him over the duration of the project would be challenging.

In hindsight, perhaps both Colin and Will were willing to collaborate with me—*but only on their terms.*

---

* Kind of like playing the game *Battleship*.

**Even small-scale collaborations can be
surprisingly cumbersome. Some people can't
or won't reimagine collaboration.**

The larger point here is that all collaborations involve different inputs and outputs. In other words, they are not all created equal, a point that my friend Dr. Terri Griffith makes in her book *The Plugged-In Manager.** At a high level, it's best to view collaborations as a continuum bounded by:

- **Long-term, high-stakes collaborations:** These key interactions require some degree of negotiation. Misunderstandings on core issues will doom the collaboration from the start. My earlier example with Colin lies on that end of the spectrum. If agreeing on a time to meet proved to be so problematic, then what were the odds that our long-term collaboration would go swimmingly well?
- **Shorter-term, low-stakes collaborations:** These light-weight, temporary, discrete, and one-off interactions ultimately don't matter all that much. As a result, they don't require much negotiation. My earlier example with Will certainly qualifies. Either one of us could have easily caved without exerting much effort.

**Be mindful of this simple model as you confront
your own inevitable collaboration challenges.**

---

* Check out her musings at *www.terrigriffith.com.*

Everyone Will Buy Into the Hub-Spoke Model of Collaboration

At its core, the model advanced in Chapter 6 is a simple one. That's not to say, however, that everyone will hop on board. Either by genuine confusion or willful ignorance, expect some folks to fight you on it.

And even if your colleagues understand it, they may actively resist adopting it. After all, change is tough.

Teams

Don't buy into the following team-related myths about reimagining collaboration.

A Team's Collaboration Cannot Improve

Our different backgrounds, personalities, genetic make-ups, and experiences invariably affect how we work and play with others. As a result, some people are inherently more collaborative than others. That's not to say, however, that we all can't improve in this critical regard.

Ask yourself the following questions:

- Are you stuck in your ways? Are your personal preferences ossified?
- Is your team collaborating more effectively than last month, last quarter, or last year? Why or why not?
- What factors are inhibiting effective collaboration?
- Does your team rely upon standalone tools, or is it moving toward the Hub-Spoke Model?

These may not be simple questions to answer. Collaborating better may require fundamental changes in your team's composition, processes, and mindset.

Collaboration Hubs Are Only for Small Teams

Tell that to IBM's top brass. In February of 2020, the tech behemoth selected Slack as its internal collaboration hub for its 350,000 employees.[3]

New Teammates Will Immediately Hit the Ground Running

Your team has used Zoom as its internal collaboration hub for years. Everyone's on-board.

Mia is her company's in-house Zoom expert. She abruptly decides to leave her job. Marsellus eventually joins the firm as her replacement. Fortunately, he's a Zoom maestro. In previous jobs, he has used Zoom channels, notifications, mentions, and all of the other bells and whistles that many people ignore.

I suspect that Marsellus will fit in nicely. Still, it will take him some time to get up to speed. For one, he needs to digest much of the content in those channels. Second, he hasn't learned the team's formal rules and informal communication and collaboration norms. (Is Jules a night person? Why does Butch use so many emojis?) Finally, he hasn't forged relationships with the others—yet.

Technology

Here are some tech-related myths about reimagining collaboration.

Hubs Guarantee Effective Collaboration

Poppycock.

Consider the following two teams:

- Team A uses an internal collaboration hub.
- Team B does not.

With no other information, which team *probably* collaborates better?

The correct answer is *Team A.*

But how can you be absolutely sure?

The example above is intentionally simplistic. In reality, effective collaboration requires more than just new applications. Think of tech as a necessary—but not sufficient—condition.

Beyond that, though, people haven't always collaborated well, even if they have used Slack, Microsoft Teams, and other hubs.

Using Slack as a Cudgel

Away is a hip, direct-to-consumer luggage brand. Its co-CEOs Steph Korey and Jen Rubio had long believed that email was ineffective for collaboration and internal communication. In its stead, the company purchased Slack.

Sounds like a collaborative and even fun place to work, right?

Not even close.

As Zoe Schiffer of *The Verge* reported in December of 2019,[4] Away's leadership:

- Banned employees from using Slack's private channels and direct messages in the name of promoting transparency.[*]
- Expected immediate responses to their queries in public channels, regardless of the time of day and day of the week.
- Lambasted employees in public Slack channels.[†]
- Made them work insane hours.
- Restricted them from taking their earned time off.
- Created a downright toxic work environment.

Knowing all of this, would you want to work at Away?

When word got out, Korey resigned her post.

Interesting postscript: She returned a few months later, ostensibly having learned her lesson.

Effective Collaboration Requires Strong Technical Chops

A pox on that statement. Sure, it might take a while to learn the ins and outs of the hubs and spokes covered in this book. What's more, there's always more to learn.

That's a far cry, however, from saying that it takes a computer-science degree to use these tools effectively.

---

[*] If you read the article, then you'll find her rationale preposterous.
[†] Read a few of her scathing messages at https://bit.ly/nog-scathing.

(I'm living proof.) If you can operate a keyboard and mouse, you'll be fine. Knowing how to drag and drop is also useful.

**Reaping the benefits from the Hub-Spoke
Model requires an open mindset, not extensive
coding experience or technical skills.**

Internal Collaboration Hubs Can Connect All Spokes

Nonsense.

Depending on the organization and the age of its different systems and applications, some spokes may be too expensive or technically difficult to connect to the hub.

Big deal.

That limitation shouldn't stop you from using Slack, Teams, Zoom, or another internal collaboration hub. Realizing the considerable benefits of hubs doesn't require complete integration.

Collaboration Hubs Immediately Transform an Organization's Culture

Say that your garden-variety Department of Motor Vehicles rolls out Slack. Within a week, Slack will immediately transform the DMV's stodgy work environment into a chic, collaborative one, right?

Don't hold your breath.

Deploying an internal collaboration hub won't suddenly repair longtime cultural fissures at your company. Rather, the tool will amplify existing workplace norms. If people acted formally at work before COVID-19, don't expect them to let their hair down in the new medium, especially at first.

Chapter Summary

- Collaboration isn't binary; there are degrees. It also may rise and drop over time.
- By itself, the use of an internal collaboration hub guarantees nothing. In fact, companies can use Slack, Zoom, and Microsoft Teams in ways that are downright abusive.
- Small-scale collaborations tend to go smoother than larger ones because fewer people are involved. Sometimes, however, even one-on-one interactions don't go as well as either party hopes. Some people will invariably refuse to reimagine collaboration.

chapter 13

Reimagining Communication and Human Resources

"If you want people to do something, make it easy. Remove the obstacles."

—RICHARD THALER

As the last chapter demonstrated, effective collaboration—remote or otherwise—is easier said than done. Its obstacles are formidable, even for organizations that have adopted the Hub-Spoke Model in earnest. New technologies can certainly help overcome them. By themselves, though, they guarantee nothing.

This chapter provides concrete steps that organizations, HR departments, managers, and rank-and-file employees can take to facilitate effective communication and collaboration.

Reimagine Employee Performance Evaluations

Does your organization, department, or manager *really* value collaboration? And how would you even know?

Rather than abstractly ponder those questions, consider the following.

At some point in your career, your manager sat you down for your annual performance appraisal. Typically about as fun as a trip to the dentist, the two of you discussed your achievements and failures* over the past year and goals for the forthcoming one.

Now think about your last assessment. Did you discuss collaboration? If so, then to what extent and in what context?

If you spent more than a few minutes on the topic, I suspect that your manager sees it as a problem and told you that you need to start playing nicer with others. You agree, but will you ultimately modify your behavior?

Say that your annual raise, bonus, and review all hinge solely upon delivering results. Will the possibility of occasionally stepping on a few toes appreciably change how you roll? In a typical organization, which sales rep would you honestly rather be?

●━━● Milquetoast Martin has never offended anyone. Last year, he booked $200,000 in sales.

---

* HR folks are fond of euphemistically rebranding these as *opportunities for improvement.*

●━━● Abrasive Alexandra sometimes rubs people the wrong way and crosses the line. Last year, the go-getter booked $1 million in sales.

Put differently, organizations and HR departments have historically viewed collaboration as a quintessential *hygiene factor*: By itself, collaborating doesn't benefit employees: no raises, promotions, or bonuses. *Failing* to collaborate, however, will certainly hurt them.

This line of thinking isn't entirely unreasonable. After all, if successfully performing a job doesn't require much collaboration, then why should managers emphasize it?

But how many jobs today fall under the umbrella of "not requiring much collaboration"? In fact, as the rising popularity of internal collaboration hubs suggests, the jobs of many, if not most, knowledge workers are becoming more collaborative.

If you accept that premise, then riddle me this: Does it make sense to continue applying individual, antiquated criteria to evaluate employee performance?

Redesign Jobs and Incentives

Let's say that your organization overhauls its performance evaluations but does nothing else. Don't expect much to happen. It's naïve to claim that rejiggering them will magically promote employee collaboration *without changing aspects of employees' underlying jobs and reward systems*.

I may have just lost you. You might be thinking that increasing collaboration necessitates making sweeping changes to your organization, department, or group.

Not necessarily.

Richard Thaler and Dan Ariely are two of the most prominent experts in the field of *behavioral economics*, one that flies in the face of long-standing economic theory. In their bestselling books, they demonstrate that human beings are *not* entirely rational. Self-interest *alone* does not drive our behavior.*

On many levels, their research has been nothing short of profound.† Governments and companies have used it to redesign systems and policies. The new ones have deliberately nudged people in particular directions. For example, Facebook nudged more than an additional 300,000 people to vote in 2010.[1]

As the following sidebar illustrates, these little tweaks can lead to plenty of other surprising changes.

How Slightly Smaller Plates Vastly Reduced Wasted Food

Thanks to the success of Airbnb, the hotel business in early 2020 faced significant challenges. And then worldwide travel nearly ground to a halt. What if hotels could reduce the amount of food that they wasted?

Steffen Kallbekken and Håkon Sælen were curious as well. The two academics ran an experiment in conjunction with 45 hotels. They wanted to know

---

* Aka *homo economicus*.
† Thaler won the 2017 Nobel Memorial Prize in Economic Sciences for his contributions to the field.

the effects of slightly reducing the plate sizes in hotel restaurants.

In June of 2013, Kallbekken and Sælen published the results of their fascinating study. The two-inch reduction reduced wasted food by as much as 22 percent.[2] Remarkably, guest satisfaction remained constant. Hotel guests barely noticed the difference.

What do plates and food waste mean for promoting effective collaboration?

Potentially, quite a bit.

The organization whose HR department treats collegiality as an afterthought on employee performance reviews is unlikely to move the collaboration needle. Instead, what if that organization did the following?

- Publicly recognized collaborative employees.
- Paid out significant monthly or quarterly awards to especially collaborative teams and employees.
- Ensured that everyone could access internal collaboration hubs.
- Endeavored to remove the technological, cultural, and logistical obstacles that inhibit effective collaboration.

Managers who are justifiably reluctant to "go big" need not be worried. As Thaler and Ariely have shown, small-scale experiments can serve as valuable, low-risk ways to gather knowledge about the impact of future changes.

If technology vastly improves, then why should jobs, processes, and performance evaluations remain the same?

Hire a Head of Remote Work

Chapter 1 covered how the tech industry has generally been ahead of the curve. Remote-first firms such as Basecamp and Automattic didn't miss a beat when COVID-19 hit. Working outside of the office was in each company's DNA.

In the wake of the pandemic, tech companies have continued to lead the pack: Along with Facebook, software companies GitLab and Okta have formalized the importance of remote work. This time, they have created new senior positions under the moniker of *Head of Remote Work*. General responsibilities of the new role include:

- Consulting upon, establishing, and enforcing policies that enable effective remote work and collaboration.
- Identifying and resolving issues that inhibit people from effectively collaborating.
- Ensuring that all employees have the tools they need to collaborate outside of the office.

Consider Quora, a 200-employee question-and-answer website.[3] On June 26, 2020, it posted a new job with the title of *Head of Remote*. Asked about the requirements for this hybrid position, CEO Adam D'Angelo said:

"You need somebody with an HR background, but they also need to be really strong at [communication skills] and to be pretty adept—or at least knowledgeable—about technology. This pandemic has forced us to just flip a switch, and now this is suddenly a role a lot of companies need."[4]

A few disclaimers are in order. First, anointing someone as grand poobah of remote work doesn't guarantee anything, including effective collaboration. Second, it's easy to dismiss this role as lip service.* Finally, because it's such a new role, the jury is still out on whether or not it will pay dividends.

Reimagine Collisions

In some ways, the transition to remote work has been relatively seamless. For example, as millions of people started working from home, Zoom, Webex, and Skype meetings largely replaced in-person ones. Other aspects of the in-person work experience, however, have been much harder to replicate in a virtual environment.

Here's how OfferUp has managed to handle this problem better than most organizations. The mobile marketplace has simulated critical, informal interactions that can establish trust—especially among new hires. What's more, it has greased the wheels for better collaboration among remote workers.

---

* Some companies faced with highly publicized scandals have reactively created the role of Chief Diversity Officer to placate their workforces and change the narrative.

Encouraging Collisions
at the Virtual Water Cooler

Without trust, effective collaboration won't take place—remote or otherwise. For many cultures, it's imperative to build trust before any business takes place. For example, in Italy and many South American countries, you'd never dream of discussing a proposal or negotiating a contract without first sharing a meal and having in-depth conversations about your family, hobbies, or even religion.

Building trust in a remote work environment can be instrumental in working better together, but it can be hard to do without intention. Consider the chance encounters that take place in physical environments—the ones that allow you to get to know your teammates:

- Waiting in line at the coffee machine
- Riding an elevator with someone

Collectively, these allow new relationships to flourish. Employees start to build familiarity and trust with one another.

Over the years, OfferUp had created a strong in-person culture. Like many companies, we struggled when COVID-19 forced us all into our homes. We wanted to recreate these serendipitous collisions—at least to the extent possible.

In April of 2020, we started using a little Slack app called Donut[5] to help facilitate chance encounters. Every Monday morning, it randomly introduces employees to new teammates, and we can easily schedule a 15-minute chat based on your shared calendar settings.

No, using Donut isn't quite the same as sharing a meal and an excellent Barolo. Still, it has proven to be a simple and fast way for our people to meet their new coworkers. As many of our employees have said in surveys, Donut has improved collaboration at OfferUp.

Natalie Angelillo is the VP of Community and Communications at OfferUp.

And Donut is hardly the only app that attempts to solve this problem. Shuffl[6] relies upon smarter sorting to go beyond randomly placing people into groups. Its matches foster meaningful online and in-person connections.

Set Core Company-Wide Hours

In Chapter 2, I delineated among three different dimensions of work:

- In-person vs. remote.
- Synchronous vs. asynchronous.
- Managers vs. makers.

Put simply and by way of review, one size doesn't fit all. Different types of activities lend themselves to different types of collaboration. It's silly to think that a company, department, or team can do everything asynchronously. Real-time communication and collaboration are essential under certain circumstances.

Many companies have squared that circle by implementing core working hours. During this period, employees must be available. For example, an organization based in the United States requires its workforce to be available from 12:30 p.m. to 4:30 p.m. EST. That way, there's a window for folks in California and New York every day to connect. Adherence to core work hours can facilitate effective collaboration by reducing the level of asynchronous work.

Reimagine Email

Chapter 4 covers the limitations of email as an internal collaboration and communication medium. Chapters 10 and 11 described some of the challenges that difficult and email-obsessed employees often pose *even after the organization adopts an internal collaboration hub.*

Employees sometimes cling to email because they know nothing else, and they fear change. Here are two powerful stratagems that companies can employ to slay the internal email beast once and for all.

Ban Internal Email

If this idea sounds radical, think again. Plenty of companies have done this and seen dramatic results.[7] My favorite example is Klick Health, an organization that eliminated email for internal communications in 1998.[8] (I detail Klick's innovative workplace in my 2015 book *Message Not Received: Why Business Communication Is Broken and How to Fix It.*)

Remove the "Reply All" Button

If banning internal email altogether is too draconian for your organization, consider removing the dreaded "reply all" button.[9] This feature was so popular and useful that Microsoft made it easier to do this in Outlook in May of 2020.[10]

Doing so forces people who want to send a message to multiple colleagues to use a different medium—ideally an internal collaboration hub.

Remember Business Processes

Chapter 10 covered several examples of inefficient and decidedly non-collaborative business processes. In each case, a little creativity and new tech resulted in more collaboration and, more important, a better business process.

That's not to say that organizations can make *all* of their business processes (more) collaborative. (No CEO wants six different employees running payroll or generating financial reports.) With the Hub-Spoke Model in mind, it's worth doing the following:

- Examining existing processes.
- Asking if there are ways to improve upon them and make them more collaborative.

Chapter Summary

- Reimagining collaboration isn't likely to happen by itself. It may require changes to existing jobs and business processes. Fortunately, they need not be big ones.

- While the jury is still out, hiring a Head of Remote Work may help increase collaboration in an organization.

- If employees won't willingly wean themselves off of email for internal communication and "collaboration," then companies can take drastic measures.

Part IV

What Now?

Chapter 14

Why Effective Collaboration Requires Lifelong Learning

> *"He knows changes aren't permanent . . .*
> *but change is."*
> —RUSH, "TOM SAWYER"

Let's say that you're a *bona fide* Slack, Microsoft Teams, or Zoom guru. Maybe your company offered a solid one week of in-depth training, and you ate it up. Alternatively, you've always had an innate ability to pick up new applications.

Either way, you know how to use every mainstream and obscure feature of one of these collaboration hubs. Your learning days are over, right?

For a few reasons, you couldn't be more wrong.

First, collaboration hubs are anything but static. On the contrary and as I can attest, they frequently add new features, tweak others, and even retire some altogether. In a similar vein, using even mature features may change if a vendor rolls out a new user interface.

Second, you may well have to learn how to use a new collaboration hub—and your employer may not provide proper training. Maybe you change jobs or pick up a new client who uses different hubs and spokes.

Finally, even if you stay in the same job, the Hub-Spoke Model isn't set in stone. Organizations sometimes change enterprise systems or adopt new ones. New third-party apps extend the power of Microsoft Teams, Zoom, and the like. New application spokes will invariably come and go.

Knowledge work requires some degree of continuous learning—and the same principle applies to collaboration. In this chapter, I'll explain how to teach yourself to become adept at these hubs and spokes while maintaining your sanity.

Ask High-Level Questions

Let's say that you want to learn how to use a new collaboration hub. The ideal process parallels the one detailed in Chapter 7.

Still, you have to be able to read the room and look beyond yourself. Consider the following questions:

- Why do you want to learn this tool?
- Does this new tool and its features make employees' lives easier?
- Are you far more tech-savvy than your colleagues?
- Do others bristle or tune out when you blather about the latest shiny new thing?
- Do they have the time or the desire to learn it?

Learning a new internal collaboration hub can be immensely rewarding. Still, for all sorts of reasons, teaching yourself how to use it effectively might not make sense. Perhaps your professional plate is already full. Alternatively, your personal situation requires you to care for a loved one in your spare time. If a tool is useful but beyond the grasp of your company or colleagues, consider whether now is the best time to learn it.

Sticking with the same hub doesn't mean that your learning days are over. Think about noodling with the following from time to time:

- New features in existing hubs.
- New spokes.
- New third-party apps.

Here's an example of the latter.

SimplePoll

Six months ago, a large PR agency deployed Slack. Employees have been faithfully using it. From time to time, they want to take each other's pulse. That is, they want to solicit quick opinions from their peers about a hodgepodge of issues. One particularly curious employee (Ann) stumbles upon SimplePoll.[1]

She should ask herself some high-level questions to evaluate its utility.

What business problem does this software application attempt to solve?

SimplePoll allows organizations to conduct—wait for it—simple polls and surveys within Slack. It also automatically tabulates and publishes the results for others to see.

What business problem does this software application not solve?

Just about everything else.

Does our company already use a similar tool that addresses the same problem?

In this case, no.[*]

If so, is the new tool appreciably better or less expensive than the incumbent?

There is no incumbent; this question is moot.

Does this app or feature make employees' lives easier?

Yes.

Is the juice worth the squeeze?

Depending on how much employees ultimately use SimplePoll, the answer is *"Yes."* SimplePoll's small-business plan is quite affordable.

---

[*] Polly is another popular polling app for Slack and Microsoft Teams, but the firm isn't currently using it.

Set Realistic Expectations

Of course, the answers to the questions in the previous sidebar need not deter you from teaching yourself a new collaboration hub or spoke. Even if there's zero chance that your employer will ultimately adopt it, you may be naturally curious or bored. Alternatively, you might be thinking of changing jobs at some point or freelancing on the side.

Still, it behooves you to check yourself at first—a mistake that I've made a few times in my career. Several times, my unbridled enthusiasm for a new application landed with a thud. My colleagues wouldn't change their ways, no matter how much I implored them. I became frustrated that they weren't picking up what I was putting down. *Why can't they see what I see?*

Watch a Short Video

You may be understandably eager to get going. (Trust me: I can relate.) Your fingers are itching to touch the keyboard and mouse. Hold off for a few minutes and watch a three- to five-minute video first. Vendor websites tend to prominently display them. Even better, take notes on the features that you find particularly interesting.

Sign Up for a Free Account

In Chapter 7, I introduced the freemium model. TL;DR: You can almost always sign up for a free account by providing minimal information—and usually not your credit card number.

Yes, doing so means that you'll receive the occasional follow-up email from the vendor, but unsubscribing is easy.

If privacy is a major concern, then just use a temporary, disposable email address.*

Start Playing

Now that you're up and running, it's time to experiment. Make mistakes. Don't worry. You won't break anything.

I am all for watching videos, but many people are kinesthetic learners: They learn by doing. What's more, don't just test the tool on a proper computer. Is there a mobile app? Is it any good?

Buy a Book

There's nothing wrong with independently experimenting with new collaboration applications and features. As I referenced in Chapter 6, plenty of free and valuable online resources make it easier than ever to pick up just about any new collaboration tool.

Some people, however, benefit from walking through a robust software application in systematic, old-school way. (Having written both *Zoom For Dummies* and *Slack For Dummies*, I'll cop to my own bias and self-interest here.†) This is especially true if you're using only one device or computer monitor.

Pace Yourself

Earlier in this chapter, I introduced SimplePoll, the very antithesis of a general-use application. It does a few things really well—and that's it.

---

* I'm a fan of https://temp-mail.org.
† I've also read my fair share of books on different applications and programming languages.

Internal collaboration hubs, however, offer far more robust functionality. As a result, you can spend a solid week delving into their robust features. Have at it if you like, but realize that you may become overwhelmed.

Don't drink from the fire hose.

Consistency Is King

I have taught quite a few software classes in my career, but one in particular sticks out.

> ### *Use It or Lose It*
>
> In 2003, I trained ten attendees at a mid-sized hospital in New Jersey in how to use their future HR and payroll system. A year or so later, the same hospital contracted me as a consultant for seven months to help them set up, test, and ultimately activate that same enterprise system. I recognized most of the folks from the previous training class.
>
> Over the course of the gig, a few of them asked me how to do something basic. I'd answer and then ask them if they remembered learning this in my class. They didn't because they hadn't touched the software since then. If you don't use it, you lose it.

The same principle holds true with collaboration tools: Consistency is king.

Say that you spend 15 minutes per day with a collaboration hub. Over two weeks, you will have played with it for three-and-a-half hours. Two things will probably have happened:

- You will retain much more of it than if you sit down for a single power session. Cramming doesn't work in the long run.[2]
- By that point, you will have grasped its essentials.

As a result, you can decide if it's worth using the hub or if you should move on.

Invite a Friend or Colleague to Experiment With You

Collaboration tools by definition don't exist in a vacuum. Yes, technically, you can use Microsoft Teams or Slack at work by yourself, but what's the point? These tools thrive when everyone in the entire company, department, or group uses them.

To this end, it's wise to bring someone else into the fray. Is one of your colleagues or friends equally curious about what the new tool can do?

If you can't find a collaboration companion, no bother. Just create an additional free account, and use it to simulate real-world collaboration. I set up about ten each while writing *Zoom For Dummies* and *Slack For Dummies*.[*]

Resist the Urge to Revert to Old Standbys

Contemporary software applications offer more-robust sharing functionality than their predecessors. (See Chapter 6 for more on this subject.) Yes, vendors occasionally and inexplicably

---

[*] I didn't want to pester my friends with a bevy of requests.

remove valuable features from their wares, but that's the exception that proves the rule.

You're probably familiar with how to accomplish a task or invoke a feature in a tried-and-true application. Case in point: Most of us know how to enable "Track Changes" in a Microsoft Word document. (I've done it more times than I can count.) As great as Word is, though, its *native* collaboration features don't compare with those of Google Docs.

If you're new to Google Docs, take a few minutes to research how to track changes in it. (Spoiler alert: It's not hard.) What's more, make sure to explain how to use this feature to others who'll be chiming in with their comments. You don't want others forking the document because they didn't realize that Google's tool does the same thing as Word, albeit just a smidge differently.

Focus, Focus, Focus

As a great deal of research suggests, toggling back and forth among different screens and apps can be jarring, introduce distractions, and ultimately inhibit long-term learning. In the words of Dr. Earl K. Miller, a prominent cognitive neuroscientist at MIT:

> People can't multitask very well, and when people say they can, they're deluding themselves. The brain is very good at deluding itself.[3]

Multitasking is really *multi-changing*. Put the phone away, close your other programs, and focus on learning the new tool.

You'll benefit far more from devoting one solid, distraction-free hour to it than you would through three hours of continuous partial attention.

Chapter Summary

- Ask yourself some key high-level questions before diving into a new collaboration hub.
- Set up a trial account (or several), and get your hands dirty.
- Focus, and try to ingest a little information at a time. Slow and steady wins the race.

chapter

The Future of Collaboration

> "Predictions are difficult,
> especially about the future."
>
> —NIELS BOHR

The last five years have brought unprecedented innovation in collaboration technology. This trend will only intensify in the coming years, and its implications for the future of work and collaboration are profound.

In this chapter, I lay out the future of work and collaboration. I then describe the specific technologies that will take us there.*

---

* For what it's worth, I have nailed many of my predictions in my last two books.

A Typical 2028 Tuesday

The year is 2028. You work at Company X as the Director of International Sales. As you'll soon see, collaboration and work in general don't resemble their 2018 counterparts.

●—●

Monday morning: You open your eyes and look at your phone. (Some things never change.) It's 7:42 a.m. Your significant other was right after all: That third glass of red last night wasn't such a good idea.

A decade ago, if you awoke so late, you would have rushed out the door in a frenzy. Your normally stressful one-hour commute would have been downright hellish.

Fortunately, it's 2028. Those days have long passed.

You don't trek into the office every day—nor do most of your colleagues for that matter. In fact, a good percentage of your peers live several hours away from Company X's nominal headquarters, often in more affordable or even exotic locales. People make the big trip every once in a while for important meetings, company pep rallies, performance reviews, and brainstorming sessions. *Where* most employees typically work, however, represents just one of many changes.

By way of background, Company X embraced the Hub-Spoke Model in early 2021. No, the shift wasn't as nearly drastic as adopting holacracy,[*] but it still required a period of adjustment.

---

[*] The radical management style eschews formal job titles, managers, and hierarchy. Companies such as Zappos have embraced it to decidedly mixed results.

On the tech side, it took a few weeks to iron out the inevitable kinks. A few of the spokes took a little effort to connect. The larger challenge was cultural: Employees had to adopt a new collaboration framework and mindset. Training helped but, as expected, a few folks clung to their ways. They ultimately decided to pursue other opportunities at more traditional companies.

Despite a few early speed bumps, the Hub-Spoke Model soon began paying dividends. Conversations moved from overflowing inboxes to more contextual, quasi-public forums. Internal email plummeted. Employees reported feeling less overwhelmed. Transparency and collaboration started to increase throughout the company. New hires weren't deluged with information on day one. The learning curve for some was nil because they came from companies that had adopted the same model, albeit with slightly different hubs and spokes.

By early 2023, the Hub-Spoke Model had surpassed the expectations of even its most ardent internal acolytes. For example, the hub learned each employee's individual work patterns, preferences, and idiosyncrasies. It became a wicked smart and indispensable work companion. You've overheard people compare themselves to Theodore, Joaquin Phoenix's character in the prescient Spike Jonze 2013 film *Her*.*

But let's get back to you.

The hub learns when and how to alert you based upon many factors, including your location. Just as important, it understands when to leave you alone. In this case, because

---

* Some *Black Mirror* episodes also come to mind.

you're working at home today, it knows that you like to get your morning run in. (In a true emergency, you'll receive a notification on your smartwatch, but we'll get back to that later.)

You power through your jog, vow to listen to your better half in the future, and rinse off. After grabbing a protein bar, you approach your computer.

You start your workday by viewing your calendar—not that you personally scheduled any of your upcoming appointments. Neither did your assistant—a job that disappeared a long time ago. When you need to meet with someone or vice-versa, the hub finds mutually convenient times for all concerned, books appointments, and reserves rooms—whether virtual, physical, or both.

The hub's increasing intelligence means that scheduling conflicts are rare. It is smart enough not to treat all requests for your time equally. Rather, the hub books appointments based upon the following factors:

- The topic of the proposed meeting.
- Whether the meeting relates to tasks that you need to complete—and when you need to complete them.
- The day of the week and the month of the year.
- The role of the person requesting your time.
- Your quarterly and monthly objectives.
- Your specific role in the company.
- The specific times that you are most productive.

The last criterion is particularly important: In your case, the hub holds the period between 1:30 and 2:30 p.m. as sacrosanct. This is a feature, not a bug. The hub learned years ago that you aren't terribly productive during that hour. After lunch, you need to recharge your batteries. You swear by your 20-minute power naps.

Your most important meeting today is set for 10:30 a.m., but there's no need to invite a notetaker. As usual, the powwow will take place in the hub whether people attend virtually or in person. It will automatically record all comments, slides, and whiteboard notes. Within 15 minutes, it will notify everyone invited that they can view accurate transcriptions and video highlights in any language they like.

You also notice a 2:30 p.m. meeting with Gary—a senior sales rep who reports to you. When not traveling, he holds his calls via Zoom.

Gary's numbers have been waning as of late, and you know exactly why: Sophisticated software reveals that he talks to prospects far more than he listens to them—a big no-no.* What's more, he ignores helpful prompts that increase the chance of closing sales by 70 percent. The hub has armed you with the right data to correct Gary's performance and help him close more sales.

Speaking of data, it permeates almost every aspect of your job. Yes, you still need to make judgment calls, but the hub provides timely analytics, dashboards, and data visualizations that inform just about all of your decisions.

Thanks to the hub, your work is qualitatively different in a few key ways. You can't recall the last time that you had to

---

* This software already exists. Check out Michael Lewis' *Against the Rules* podcast at bit.ly/11-lewis-sales.

hunt down basic product, employee, or vendor information. Ditto for asking colleagues to send you a spreadsheet. You can quickly and securely access all enterprise information without leaving the hub.

Sure, you still need to search for information from time to time, but the process takes a fraction of the time compared to the pre-hub days. For example, on Wednesday you need to find an employee with a very specific set of skills, to paraphrase Liam Neeson's frequently imitated *Taken* line. Ten years ago, you would send a mass email or maybe post a message on the company intranet.

You wouldn't dream of doing either thing today. You simply speak into your nearest device. Within seconds, the hub recommends the top three people at Company X who can help you. It also sets up 30-minute appointments with each of them.

You still check your inbox, but only a few times per day. In fact, you can't remember the last time that you received an email from a colleague.

This is just one example of how the hub saves you time. Here's another. The hub has allowed Company X to automate large functions within its enterprise-resource planning and customer-relationship management systems. Long gone are the days of toggling back and forth among eight different places to approve requisitions, expense reports, invoices, and employee vacation requests. Ditto for updating customer information and providing quotes. You do all of those things—and more—in a single place: the hub. To say that it has simplified internal business processes is the acme of understatement.

The hub is no one-trick pony. It also serves as a high-tech radar or smoke detector for latent issues. It knows which matters are truly *urgent*—and not because a colleague sent you a late-night message containing that hackneyed corporate word. On occasion, it evens ping you during your afternoon snooze.

Beyond notifications for specific events, the hub provides valuable general advice on how to do your job in a timely manner. It even nudges you in subtle ways, as discussed in Chapter 11. It gives you answers to questions that you didn't even think to ask. Years ago, you marveled at these insightful and eerily relevant suggestions. Now, you take them for granted.

The hub recommends relevant industry and management articles that you would otherwise miss—and adds them to your customized feed. For instance, before an upcoming series of performance reviews, it suggests new research on the best way to hold difficult conversations with Millennials who aren't making the grade.

In short, the hub changed everything.

Emerging Technologies

A bevy of powerful technologies is poised to make today's collaboration hubs look like child's play. Here are the most critical ones.

Artificial Intelligence and Machine Learning

In a word, software and machines are becoming smarter. Much, much smarter.

Picture the following simple yet über-useful scenario.

You take a one-week vacation and go completely off the grid. Your company buys into the Hub-Spoke Model. As a result, you use Microsoft Teams in lieu of email, but, in a way, you're still worried: You'll still have to review thousands of messages when you return. But which ones are critical? And how long will it take you to find them?

Hubs will largely answer those questions for you. Over time, they will learn which messages to prioritize—and not by searching for simple keywords. They will apply different criteria to different people, roles, and departments. They'll also factor in the times of the day, days of the week, and the times of the year.

Oh, and they'll learn your work preferences. They'll know when you are most productive and when you need a break. They will automatically adjust the frequency, timing, and types of notifications accordingly.

Companies are planting these seeds right now. On October 21, 2020, the project-management tool Wrike announced powerful new AI and ML tools to keep projects on track.[1] At a high level, the new features will help predict project risks, prioritize specific tasks, and expedite project completion.

Better Analytics

Hubs will provide greater insights into how we work, many of which remain hidden.[*] It's not a matter of *if*; it's a matter of *when*.

---

[*] I saw this enhancement coming a mile away. I made that very prediction in November of 2019, when I was finishing the *Slack For Dummies* manuscript.

Case in point: At Slack's Frontiers conference on October 6, 2020, CEO Stewart Butterfield announced that the company was building tools that measured fuzzy things, such as levels of internal collaboration and workforce engagement.[2]

Increased Automation

Internal collaboration hubs and their spokes will rely more and more upon bots and increased automation. If you haven't heard of *robotic process automation* yet, you will.

Software will automatically handle most of the tasks that we do manually today. Examples include processing healthcare and insurance claims, pulling price data from websites, and routing customer requests in call centers.[3]

Better and Deeper Voice Integration

Amazon Echo, Google Home, and Apple's Siri represent three of the most popular ways that untold millions of consumers interact with their devices by speaking to them. Expect all of today's collaboration hubs to start providing similar functionality.

As it is, you can already talk to dedicated Zoom appliances.[4] Zoom's live translations let people chat, even if they speak different languages.[5] The power, accuracy, and applicability of voice will vastly improve over the next decade.

Augmented Reality and Virtual Reality

What if videoconferencing *really* resembled the real world?

In July of 2020, Microsoft announced the launch of a new Teams feature designed to "give people the impression that everyone is looking at the entire group in a big virtual mirror."[6] Dubbed *Together Mode*, it would ostensibly alleviate the problems that plague traditional videoconferencing tools. That is, it will reduce Zoom fatigue.

FIGURE 15.1: Microsoft Teams' Together Mode

Not to be outdone, Zoom soon followed suit. On October 14, 2020, the company announced Immersive Scenes—its answer to Microsoft's Together Mode.* [7]

Much like voice, software vendors are bringing long-hyped AR and VR to their products. Again, the question is when—not if—these features arrive. Expect the lines between the virtual and physical worlds to get even blurrier.

Internal Collaboration Hubs Will Continue Opening Up

It's easy to invite non-employees to internal collaboration hubs as guests, but we're just getting started. Vendors are building private, secure tunnels that connect different

---

* To watch a demo of this feature, visit bit.ly/nog-tog-mode.

organizations' hubs. At present, Slack leads the pack here with Slack Connect.[8] Expect the other deep-pocketed vendors to catch up—and fast.

In fact, this is already happening. Researching this book, I spoke to Vlad Shlosberg, CEO at Foqal. His startup centralizes customer-support requests within Slack.

Shlosberg relayed a story about a tech company in Manhattan that was struggling with its customer service. Frustration abounded: Customers were spending hours asking basic questions to resolve their issues.

Foqal built a custom spoke for its client: A nifty Slack button that allowed its customers to initiate queries within the hub. After they clicked the button, their help requests entered a centralized queue.

Within two weeks, first-response times dropped from hours to seconds. Leadership gained valuable insights into how its customers felt. Oh, and customer satisfaction clocked in at 93 percent.

New Players Will Shake Things Up

When it comes to collaboration hubs, Microsoft, Slack, Zoom, Google, Facebook, and other large tech firms will drive a great deal of innovation. If you think that aspiring, smaller companies are standing still, though, think again.

For example, the startup MURAL announced that it raised $118 million in additional funding.[9] The company provides a whiteboard-like digital environment that lets users collaborate and brainstorm wherever they are. All Turtles' mmhmm app, Here.fm, and Loom.ai are some other interesting newcomers to the collaboration-tech party. Expect many more. Apart from creating new and useful features, these upstarts will force the established players to keep innovating. The arms race shows no signs of abating.

Beyond Technology

In researching this book, I've come to an unmistakable conclusion: the world of work will never return to its pre-pandemic state. The future of work resembles the future of both healthcare and education: All three will be hybrid.

Consider "The State of Remote Work," an in-depth report published by OwlLabs in October 2020.[10] Among its notable findings:

- Despite difficult circumstances for working remotely, 77 percent of respondents agree that, after COVID-19, having the option to work from home would make them happier.
- Four in five full-time workers expect to work from home at least three days per week after COVID-19 guidelines are lifted and companies are able to reopen their doors.

As we've seen throughout this book, collaboration technologies are mature enough to support permanent remote work, even at a massive scale. What's more, as OwlLabs' research suggests, people clearly prefer not having to slog to an office every day.

Additional data from Gallup confirms our preferences:

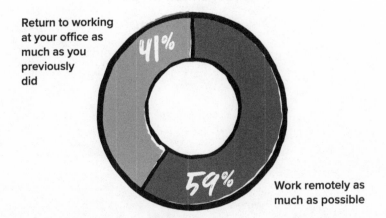

**Workers Taking to
Remote Work Amid COVID-19 Crisis**

Once restrictions on businesses and school closures are lifted,
if your employer left it up to you, would you prefer to:

Return to working
at your office as
much as you
previously
did

41%

59%

Work remotely as
much as possible

Source: Gallup Panel, 2020. Based on U.S. workers who are
working from home as a result of COVID-19.

FIGURE 15.2: Breakdown of Employee Work Preferences

Most employees will eventually return to their offices—just
not on a full-time basis. At a high level, the future of knowledge
work will look much more like 2020 than 2000. By extension,
the need to reimagine collaboration will only increase.

Chapter Summary

●━● Collaboration hubs will become smarter, more automated, and more immersive in the coming years.

- Plenty of innovation and useful collaboration features will stem from upstarts.
- The future of work will be more remote and collaborative than its past. The sooner you and your colleagues realize it, the better off you will all be.

Chapter 16

Recommendations for Reimagining Collaboration

"Some men you just can't reach."
—CAPTAIN, ROAD PRISON 36, *Cool Hand Luke*

This final chapter distills some of the most important advice in this book into a number of concrete and pragmatic suggestions.

No, the following tips don't represent a comprehensive checklist to ensure effective collaboration. You can follow all of them and still experience problems working with your colleagues for all sorts of peripheral reasons. *All else being equal*, though, companies, departments, groups, and individuals adhering to them are more likely to:

- Collaborate more effectively.
- Waste less time.
- Get more out of their collaboration tech.
- Improve their group and individual results.

1. Know Thyself

Using hubs and spokes is not a binary. An organization falls into one of the following four levels described in Table 16.1:

Level	Description
0	It exclusively uses email for internal "collaboration." In other words, it is stuck in the 1990s.
1	It has deployed an internal collaboration hub, but employees use it inconsistently and only as Email 2.0. No one has connected any spokes to the hub.
2	It has deployed an internal collaboration hub and connected some spokes, but employee usage remains sporadic, perhaps confined to a few progressive departments or groups.
3	It has deployed an internal collaboration hub and connected as many spokes as possible. Employee usage is universal.

TABLE 16.1: Collaboration Maturity Model

Understanding this simple framework is essential: It's nearly impossible to skip levels. For example, a firm isn't going to jump from Level 0 to Level 2.

Another golf analogy is in order: You aren't going to break 80 if you've never cracked 100.

2. Ditch Internal Email for Good

The second tip is arguably the most important one. Sure, you may be able to complete a simple task with someone else over email from time to time. Reverting to your inbox, however, subtly thwarts efforts to imbue a culture of collaboration throughout the organization.

> **Effective, long-term collaboration cannot take place via email. Period.**

3. Go All-In on a Single Hub

As useful as internal collaboration hubs and their spokes are, senior leadership or your manager may not compel all employees to use them. As a result, the level of collaboration within the organization will suffer. Organizations that take half measures will see only a fraction of the benefits of going all-in.

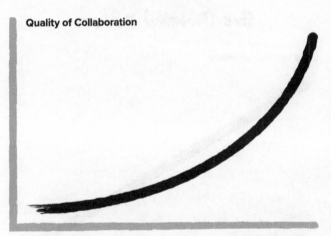

Tools Matter

Quality of Collaboration

Proportion of Employees in the Organization Who Use Collaboration Hubs

FIGURE 16.1: Tools Matter

> **The more that a team or organization embraces the Hub-Spoke Model, the better its collaboration will be.**

4. Remember That Everything Is Connected

Internal collaboration hubs make it far easier for people to work together. The mere presence of these tools, however, doesn't guarantee anything. Employees who replicate old, inefficient habits and ignore changing antiquated business processes won't realize the full benefits of the Hub-Spoke Model.

> Reimagining collaboration requires more than just using new tools. It also requires adopting a new mindset.

5. Remember That Size (Probably) Matters

Equipped with no other information, I'd wager that a five-employee law firm collaborates better than its 3,000-employee counterpart.

Size (Probably) Matters

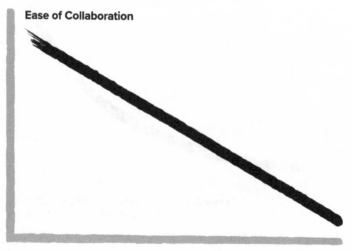

Ease of Collaboration

Number of Employees in the Organization

FIGURE 16.2: Size (Probably) Matters

As the number of employees in an organization increases, adopting the Hub-Spoke Model becomes more difficult.

6. Be Patient (Up to a Point)*

During my tenure at ASU, I explained Slack to a curious colleague and friend of mine. It took him all of about four minutes to get it. He had worked with similar applications before. In no time, he was using it in his classes in lieu of email.

It's unreasonable to expect everyone in your organization to *immediately* grasp the intricacies of internal collaboration hubs, never mind change their entrenched habits and redesign tried-and-true business processes.* On the other hand, it's equally ridiculous to pooh-pooh an aloof peer who attempts to move internal discussions from Zoom to email for the fifteenth time.

Be patient with your colleagues as they learn new collaboration tools—up to a point.

7. Be Curious

Let's say that you regularly use two applications. Ask yourself a simple question: Either directly or through an internal collaboration hub, can you connect them? And how much work would that entail?

As the following sidebar shows, the answers may surprise you.

---

* Particularly at large organizations.

Connecting Unfamiliar Spokes

I contracted a small business last year. Its founder Jordan (a pseudonym) used 17hats for customer-relationship management and Wrike for project management. I had heard of both tools before but had never used either one.

Within the first few hours of our engagement, two things happened. First, I started receiving a flurry of emails. (That was a quick fix. I installed the Wrike app for Slack[1] and disabled its email notifications.)

Second, I realized that Jordan hadn't stitched together 17hats and Wrike. It seemed inefficient to key information into both systems. Plus, it wouldn't take long for one of them to get out of sync with the other—something that no small business owner wants.

A quick Google search revealed what I had suspected: Zapier would allow Jordan to easily connect 17hats with Wrike.[2] No coding required.

I sent Jordan the URL. She installed that particular Zap[*] and *voilà!* She had connected the two tools. At that point, the Hub-Spoke Model really hit home for her.

A simple Google search may save you hours of time.

---

[*] Not be confused with Zoom's Zapps, mentioned in Chapter 6.

8. Call Bullshit on Collaboration Kabuki Theater

Embracing the Hub-Spoke Model certainly makes effective collaboration easier. Again, however, there are no guarantees. Consider the following scenarios:

- Incessantly debating topics via Slack direct messages or in private Microsoft Teams channels.
- Responding to others' comments in a Google Doc *ad nauseam*.
- Deciding in advance on a key policy decision and using the hub to shape the argument toward the predetermined conclusion.

Remember from Chapter 2 that certain types of tasks and projects are best suited for synchronous communication and collaboration.

Just because the discussion or task takes place in a hub doesn't mean that it's truly collaborative.

9. Know When to Walk Away

Chapter 11 detailed seven examples of employees who, either intentionally or not, didn't collaborate well with their colleagues, partners, and vendors. When these people and situations present themselves, you can take one of three paths:

1. Weather the storm, and continue as is. Maybe you have reached the point of no return.[*]

2. Attempt to change the situation or alter the person's behavior. In these cases, try to be measured. A tactful, real-time conversation is more likely to pay dividends than sending a cold or scolding message.

3. Realize that your current situation is untenable and consider folding your hand. Doing so might cause you some short-term financial and/or professional hardship. Still, it may represent your best long-term move.

If a profound lack of collaboration consistently impedes your performance, project, or career, consider cutting bait and moving on.

Chapter Summary

- Just because you use a hub and embrace the Hub-Spoke Model doesn't ensure seamless collaboration. I like your odds, though.
- The larger the organization, the harder it will be for its employees to embrace new tools and, by extension, collaborate effectively. Realize this going in.
- Be patient with employees—up to a point. No one should get unlimited bites at the collaboration apple.

---

[*] Professional poker players call this being *pot committed.*

Conclusion and Parting Words

In the classic 1999 film *The Matrix*, Laurence Fishburne's enigmatic character Morpheus says to Keanu Reeves's Neo:

> This is your last chance. After this, there is no going back. You take the blue pill, and the story ends. You wake up in your bed and you believe whatever you want to believe. You take the red pill, and you stay in Wonderland, and I show you how deep the rabbit hole goes. Remember that all I am offering is the truth. Nothing more.[*]

In a similar vein, you may find yourself at a similar crossroads. Fortunately, you have now gained new insights about how to effectively collaborate. Equipped with this knowledge, you can open your mind to exciting and decidedly more collaborative ways of working. You can embrace these new possibilities. You can nudge your colleagues to do the same.

---

[*] Watch the scene yourself at https://bit.ly/nog-matrix.

When you do, you'll position yourself as a force for change within your organization.

Or . . .

You can cling to antiquated tools and habits. You can resist change, maybe even for five or ten years. Put differently, I can't stop you from taking the blue pill.

But I hope you take the red one.

Thank-You

*"To defend what you've written
is a sign that you are alive."*
—WILLIAM ZINSSER

Thank you for buying *Reimagining Collaboration*. I hope that you have enjoyed the preceding pages. Ideally, you have found this book informative, and it has challenged your assumptions about work. Its advice and knowledge will help you achieve your professional goals. And perhaps you are willing to help me.

Doing each of these things is helpful:

- Writing a book review on amazon.com, bn.com, goodreads.com, and/or your blog. The more honest, the better.
- Mentioning the book on Facebook, Reddit, Twitter, Quora, LinkedIn, and other sites you frequent.
- Recommending it to anyone who might find it interesting.
- Giving it as a gift.
- Checking out my other books at *www.philsimon.com/books*.

I write books for several reasons. First, that's just what a writer does. Second, I believe that I have something meaningful to say about an important topic. Next, I like writing, editing, crafting a cover, and everything else that goes into writing books. To paraphrase the title of an album by Geddy Lee, it's my favorite headache.

Although Kindles, Nooks, and iPads are downright cool, I enjoy holding a physical copy of one of my books in my hands. In our digital world, creating something tangible from scratch just feels good to me. Fourth, I find writing to be incredibly cathartic. Finally, writing books opens professional doors for me.

At the same time, though, producing a quality text takes an enormous amount of time, effort, and money. Every additional copy sold helps make the next one possible.

Let me know if I can help your company, department, or group collaborate better.

Phil Simon
www.philsimon.com
January 1, 2021

Suggested Reading

Ariely, Dan. *Predictably Irrational, Revised and Expanded Edition: The Hidden Forces That Shape Our Decisions.* Harper Perennial, 2009.

Berkun, Scott. *The Year Without Pants: WordPress.com and the Future of Work.* Jossey-Bass, 2013.

Csikszentmihalyi, Mihaly. *Flow: The Psychology of Optimal Experience.* Harper Perennial, 2008.

Fried, Jason, and Hansson, David Heinemeier. *Remote: Office Not Required.* Currency, 2013.

Fried, Jason, and Hansson, David Heinemeier. *Rework.* Currency, 2010.

Galloway, Scott. *Post Corona: From Crisis to Opportunity.* Portfolio, 2020.

Griffith, Terri. *The Plugged-In Manager: Get in Tune with Your People, Technology, and Organization to Thrive.* Jossey-Bass, 2011.

Lencioni, Patrick. *The Five Dysfunctions of a Team: A Leadership Fable*. Jossey-Bass, 2011.

Newport, Cal. *Deep Work: Rules for Focused Success in a Distracted World*. Grand Central Publishing, 2016.

Stone, Brad. *The Everything Store: Jeff Bezos and the Age of Amazon*. Hachette, 2013.

Thaler, Richard, and Sunstein, Cass R. *Nudge: Improving Decisions About Health, Wealth, and Happiness*. Penguin, 2009.

Acknowledgments

For making this book happen: Michele DeFilippo, Ronda Rawlins, Frank Kresen, Kathryn Lloyd, Karen Davis, Luke Fletcher, and Johnna VanHoose Dinse.

A tip of the hat to the people who keep me grounded and listen to my rants: Dalton Cervo, Rob Hornyak, Hina Arora, Daniel Teachey, Steve Putnam, Emily Freeman, Chris Olsen, Greg Dawson, Steve Katz, Michael Viola, Joe Mirza, Dave Sandberg, Chris McGee, Scott Berkun, Josh Bernoff, Alan Berkson, Andrew Botwin, John Andrewski, Jennifer Zito, Thor Sandell, Rob Metting, Prescott Perez-Fox, Jason Horowitz, Mike Frutiger, Marc Paolella, Peter and Hope Simon, Jennie Grossberg, Mark Cenicola, Helen Thompson, Sarah Garcia, Jason Conigliari, JR Camillon, Daniel Green, Matt Wagner, and Brian and Heather Morgan.

My conversations with the following peeps made this book richer: Terri Griffith, Mike Vardy, Natalie Angelillo, Brian Sommer, Laurie Feuerstein, Lowell Vande Kamp, Christina Meng, Niels Larson, Tylar Dykman, Mandy Yeung Garby, Matthew Lee, Will Sanders, Rohit Bhargava, Marnie McMahon, Jessica Angerstein, Mariko Hewer, and especially my *consigliere* Alan Simon.

Nietzsche once said, "Without music, life would be a mistake."

He wasn't wrong.

For decades of incredible music, thank you to the members of Rush (Geddy, Alex, and Neil), Marillion (h, Steve, Ian, Mark, and Pete), and Dream Theater (Jordan, John, John, Mike, and James). Your songs continue to inspire millions of discerning fans. I am proud to call myself one of them.

Vince Gilligan, Peter Gould, Bryan Cranston, Aaron Paul, Dean Norris, Anna Gunn, Bob Odenkirk, Betsy Brandt, Jonathan Banks, Giancarlo Esposito, RJ Mitte, Michael Mando, Rhea Seehorn, Michael McKean, Patrick Fabian, Tony Dalton, and the rest of the *Breaking Bad* and *Better Call Saul* teams have inspired me to do great work.

Finally, to my family: Thank you.

About the Author

Phil Simon is a frequent keynote speaker, dynamic trainer, recognized collaboration and technology authority, and college professor-for-hire. He is the award-winning author of ten previous books, including *The Age of the Platform: How Amazon, Apple, Facebook, and Google Have Redefined Business* and *Message Not Received: Why Business Communication Is Broken and How to Fix It*. He advises organizations on how to communicate, collaborate, and use technology. Simon's contributions have appeared in the *Harvard Business Review*, *The New York Times*, CNBC, and on many other prominent media outlets. He also hosts the podcast *Conversations About Collaboration*.

Simon holds degrees from Carnegie Mellon University and Cornell University.

Learn more about him and his work at *www.philsimon.com*.

Index

#

17hats, 226
37signals, 7

A

ActivTrak, 11
Agile Method, implementation, 135–136
Agilefall, 135
aging in reverse, 75
AI (artificial intelligence), 213–214
Airtable, 90
analytics, 214–215
Andreessen, Marc, 5
APIs (application programming interfaces), 71–72
applications, multiple, 80–84
Arizona State University, xxi
Asana, 76, 82, 150
asynchronous collaboration, 40
asynchronous communications, 170, 227
asynchronous work, 5, 35–36
Atom, 82

audience, xxviii
automation, 74, 215
Automattic, 7–8

B

Baer, Jay, 80–81
Basecamp, 76, 82
behavioral economics, 186
Benjamin Button Economy, 75
Berkun, Scott, 8
Berners-Lee, Tim, 5
Bina, Eric, 5
blind spots, 48
book publishing, 145–150, 171–172
bottom-up approach to implementation, 130–131
Brave, 81
Breaking Bad, 140

C

Calendly, 150
Canva, 81, 94–95, 150
Cashman, Paul M., 36
change resistance, 118–120

Cisco Webex, 69
cloud computing, 102
CodePen, 82
cognitive load
  e-commerce and, 58
  email and, 56–57
collaboration
  asynchronous work, 5
  communication, 20–21
  company size, 224–225
  as continuum, 175
  dimensions, 36
  elusiveness of, 8–12
  future of
    AI (artificial intelligence),
      213–214
    analytics, 214–215
    augmented reality,
      215–216
    automation, 215
    ML (machine learning),
      213–214
    new options, 217–218
    scenario, 208–213
    virtual reality, 215–216
    voice integration, 215
    workplace, 218
  history, 3–4
    office-based, 4–5
  Hub-Spoke model, 85–88
  limitations, 32–33
  location, 33–34
  mindset changes, 224

  spokes and, 93–96
  synchronous work, 5
  talent pools and, 14
  trust building, 190–191
collaboration hubs. See inter-
    nal collaboration hubs
Collaboration Maturity Model,
  222
collaboration tools, forced
    adoption and, 9–10
collisions, 189–191
communication, 28
  asynchronous, 170, 227
  collaboration and, 20–21
  definition, 20–22
  synchronous, 170, 227
commute time, remote work
  and, 9
company-wide hours, 191–192
Conversations About Collab-
  oration podcast, 81
Convince and Convert
  Consulting, 80–81
cooperation, 22–23, 28
cooperative work, 36
coordination, 23, 29
core working hours, 191–192
corporate real-estate expenditures, 15
costs, 123–124
Coursera, 93
COVID-19
  city population changes, 13

remote work and, 12–13
reporting, software limita-
    tions, 118
universities, xxii–xxiii
creativity, 38
CSCW (computer-supported
    cooperative work), 36
customer retention, 49

D

Dashlane, 82
decentralized approach to
    implementation, 130–131
deep work, 27, 31
delegation, 23, 29
Discord, 69
distributed companies, 6–8
DocuSign, 150
Donut, 190–191
Doodle, 150
Dropbox, 77, 82

E

e-commerce, cognitive load
    and, 58
economics law of diminishing
    returns, 105
email
  alternatives, 58–59
  cognitive load and, 56–57
  versus collaboration hubs,
      55, 57
  critical context, 56–58

employees leaving, 53
internal, 192–193, 222–223
network effect, 52
organizational knowledge
    and, 53–54
recalling messages, 55
Reply All, 193
employees
  impatience, 119–120
  incentives, 185–188
  learning curve, 119–120
  performance evaluations,
      184–185
  resistance, 118–119
  retention, 49
  training, 120–121
employee-surveillance soft-
    ware, remote work
    and, 11
enterprise search and retrieval,
    46–47
enterprise technology, adop-
    tion field color, 112
Epp, Larson, 16–17
Expensify, 142–143

F

Facebook, Workplace, 68
fast-follower strategy, 70
Feedly, 82
fields of enterprise technology
    adoption, 112
Figma, 94–95

food waste, 186–187
Formscape, 90
Freedom, 76
freemium business model, 102
Fubini, Eugene, xx
future of collaboration
  AI (artificial intelligence), 213–214
  analytics, 214–215
  augmented reality, 215–216
  automation, 215
  ML (machine learning), 213–214
  new options, 217–218
  scenario, 208–213
  virtual reality, 215–216
  voice integration, 215
  workplace, 218

G

Galloway, Scott, 75
GarageBand, 82
GitLab, 188
Glitch, 66
Google
  Docs, 171
  Meet, Zoom breakout rooms, 107
  Tasks, 76
  Workspace, 69, 81
Graham, Paul, 38
Greif, Irene, 36

H

Hansson, David Heinemeier, 7
Head of Remote Work, 188–189
Hub-Spoke Model, 85–88
  benefits, 95–96
  bridges, 91
  business processes
    book publishing, 145–150
    employee expense submission, 140–143
    technical issues, 143–145
  connecting spokes, 226
  future scenario, 208–213
  limitations, 96
  resistance, scenarios, 154–164
  trust building, 190–191
  vendors, 113
human resources, 184–185
hybrid work arrangements, 16

I

IFTTT (If This Then That), 90
Immersive Scenes (Zoom), 216
iMovie, 82
impatience of employees, 119–120
implementation
  Agile Method, 135–136
  bottom-up approach, 130–131

change resistance, 118–119
costs, 123–124
decentralized approach, 130–131
leadership and, 120–122
learning curve, 119–120
middle-out approach, 133–134
organizational politics and, 124–125
Phased Gate Method, 135–136
top-down approach, 131–133
training, 120–121
Waterfall Method, 135–136
information location, 46–47
internal collaboration hubs, xvii. *See also* Hub-Spoke Model
aging in reverse, 75
all-in adoption, 223
automation, 74
company culture and, 111
compliance, 110
definition, 65
diminishing returns, 104–106
Discord, 69
economics and, 104–106
versus email, 55, 57
employee flexibility and, 111
external organizations, 114
integration, 71, 108–109

knowledge management, 73
learning new, 198–206
Microsoft Teams, 66–67
multiple, 102–104
regulations, 110
security, 110–111
selecting
cost, 108
questions to ask, 100–101
vendor relationships, 108
single best myth, 106–107
Slack, 66
smartphones and, 74
stability and, 110
switching, 113–114
vendor size and, 110
Webex, 69
Workplace, 68
Zoom, 67–68
Internet, early years, 5–6
Internet Relay Chat, 63
interoperability, 84
IRC (Internet Relay Chat), 63
IT issues, 143–145

J
job redesign, 185–188

K
knowledge flow, 45

L

labor costs, remote work and, 14–15
law of diminishing returns, 105
leadership commitment, 120–122
learning curve, 119–120
learning new collaboration hubs, 198–200
  books, 202
  consistency, 203–204
  expectations, 201
  experimenting, 202, 204
  free accounts, 201–202
  multi-tasking, 205–206
  progress, 202–203
  reverting to old ways, 205
  video resources, 201
LinkedIn, 82
LinkedIn Learning, 93

M

manager *versus* maker, 38
The Matrix, 229
meetups, 93
Microsoft
  Office, 81
  Power Automate, 88
  SharePoint, 66
  Teams, 66–67, 81, xvii, xxv
    Together Mode, 216
  Yammer, 66

middle-out approach to implementation, 133–134
Mio, 103–104
Machine learning, 213–214
Morgenfeld, Todd, 14
Mosaic Web browser, 5
Mullenweg, Matt, 7–8
multitasking, 30
  definition, 26
  learning new collaboration hub, 205–206
myths about collaboration
  general, 168–176
  teams, 176–177
  technology, 178–180

N

network effect of email, 52
Newport, Cal, 27

O

OfferUp, 189–191
Okta, 188
OneDrive, 82
OnwardMobility, 33
organizational blind spots, 48
organizational health, 47–48
organizational knowledge, email and, 53–54
organizational productivity, 45–46

P

PDFPen, 82
Phased Gate Method of implementation, 135–136
Pocket, 82
politics, implementation and, 124–125
Power Automate (Microsoft), 88
   template, 89
privacy, 122–123
productivity, 23–26, 30
   organizational, 45–46
   team, 45–46
project management, 27, 32

Q

Quora, 93, 188–189

R

Reddit, 93
remote work, 31
   commute time and, 9
   corporate real-estate expenditures, 15
   COVID-19 and, 12–13
   definition, 27
   distributed companies, 6–8
   employee-surveillance software, 11
   forced adoption, 16–17
   Head of Remote Work position, 188–189
   hybrid work arrangements, 16
   labor costs and, 14–15
   management's trust in employees, 11–12
   percent increase in 2020, 10
   rocket surgeons, 111

S

SaaS (software-as-service), 72–73, 102
Safari, 81
scheduling, 172
SDKs (software development kids), 72
security, 122–123
shadow IT, 102–103
SharePoint, 66
Shuffl, 191
SimplePoll, 199–200
Skype, 66
Slack, 66, 81, xvii, xxv
   channels, 57
   Connect, 217
   DocuSign, 150
   Donut, 190–191
   Expensify and, 142–143
   university use, xxiv–xxv
   Workflow Builder, 89
   Wrike, 226
   Zendesk and, 145

Zoom and, 109
Slack For Dummies, xix
smartphones, 74
Smartsheet, 76
spokes, 65, 76, 84, xvii
   Asana, 76
   Basecamp, 76
   Canva, 94–95
   Dropbox, 77
   enterprise systems, 77
   Figma, 94–95
   Freedom, 76
   Google Tasks, 76
   Smartsheet, 76
   Todoist, 76, 94
   Toggl, 76
   Trello, 76
   Workspace, 76
   Wrike, 76
Spotify, 95
StackExchange, 93
step changes, 99
Sucoco, 81
synchronous communications, 170, 227
synchronous work, 5, 35–36

T

Tableau, 82
team productivity, 45–46
teams, collaboration myths, 176–177
Teamwork, 81

technology, collaboration myths, 178–180
technology costs, 123–124
The Everything Store, 96
Todoist, 76, 82, 94
Together Mode (Microsoft Teams), 216
Toggl, 76
top-down approach to implementation, 131–133
training, 120–121
transparency, 44
Trello, 76, 82, 150
trust among employees, 49
Twitter, 82

U

Udemy, 93

V

Vidyard, 81
virtual reality, 215–216
voice integration, 215

W

Waterfall Method of implementation, 135–136
WaveApps, 82
Wave.video, 82
Webex, 69
webhooks, 72
WordPress, 7–8, 82
Workato, 90

working hours, 191–192
Workplace (Facebook), 68
Workspace (Google), 69, 76,
      81
World Wide Web, 5
Wrike (Slack), 76, 226

Y

Yammer, 66
YouCanBook.me, 150, 172
  sample, 173
YouTube, 93

Z

Zapier, 90
Zapps, 84, 85
Zendesk, 144–145
Zoom, 67–68, 81, xvii, xxv
  breakout rooms, Google
      Meet and, 107
  growth, 67
  Immersive Scenes, 216
  Slack and, 109
  Zapps, 84, 85
Zoom For Dummies, xix
Zoomtopia, 84–85

Endnotes

Introduction

1. https://bit.ly/asu-int-5
2. https://bit.ly/one-in-five-asu
3. https://bit.ly/asu-fees-x
4. https://bit.ly/nog-asu
5. https://www.asu.edu
6. https://bit.ly/nyt-china-covid
7. https://bit.ly/nog-asu3
8. https://bit.ly/nog-asu4

Chapter 1

1. Source: Economic Research Service, United States Department of Agriculture. https://bit.ly/3mfNhZl
2. https://bit.ly/nog-35-wp
3. https://bit.ly/simon-39-wp
4. https://bit.ly/nog-fp.
5. https://bit.ly/nog-surv
6. https://bit.ly/nog-LTremote
7. https://bit.ly/nog-pint
8. https://bit.ly/nog-desmoines
9. https://bit.ly/nog-menlo
10. https://bit.ly/nog-wages
11. https://bit.ly/nog-space

Chapter 2

1. https://bit.ly/2YvZWNB
2. https://bit.ly/nog-simon27

Chapter 3

1. https://bit.ly/nog-simon1
2. https://bit.ly/nog-tsia
3. https://bit.ly/nog-forr
4. bit.ly/findwise-sl
5. https://mck.co/31lof2B

Chapter 4

1. https://mck.co/2NhRP1G
2. https://bit.ly/nog-cog

Chapter 5

1. https://bit.ly/simon-nog3
2. https://bit.ly/nog-slack-buy
3. https://bit.ly/nog-slack1
4. https://bit.ly/nog-zoom
5. https://bit.ly/nog-baffling
6. https://bit.ly/nog-car
7. https://bit.ly/nog-button
8. https://bit.ly/nog-drop

Chapter 6

1. https://www.philsimon.com/podcast/episode-1-jay-baer/
2. https://bit.ly/hsc-zapps

3. https://bit.ly/nog-slackwf
4. https://bit.ly/nog-slack-wf
5. https://bit.ly/nog-weather
6. https://bit.ly/nog-ifttt2
7. https://bit.ly/nog-ifttt

Chapter 7

1. bit.ly/sl-mil
2. https://bit.ly/nog-water
3. http://bit.ly/nog-sl-zm
4. https://bit.ly/nog-slackc

Chapter 8

1. https://bit.ly/nog-excel
2. https://bit.ly/nog-army
3. https://on.wsj.com/2kNjuMP

Chapter 10

1. https://on.wsj.com/2Gmyzjc
2. http://bit.ly/nog-exp
3. http://bit.ly/zdslack
4. https://bit.ly/nog-docusign
5. https://bit.ly/nog-docusign
6. https://www.recruitingfromscratch.com

Chapter 11

1. https://bit.ly/hub-healthcare

Chapter 12

1. https://bit.ly/nog-vidcall
2. https://bit.ly/nog-3em
3. https://bit.ly/yeah-ibm
4. http://bit.ly/bad-slack

Chapter 13

1. https://bit.ly/nog-fb-vote
2. https://bit.ly/nog-nudge
3. https://workew.com/job/head-of-remote-quora
4. https://wapo.st/2GKaJgY
5. https://www.donut.com
6. https://shuffl.ai
7. https://bit.ly/2GP9QUn
8. https://bit.ly/nog-click
9. https://bit.ly/nog-r-all
10. https://bit.ly/nog-rall2

Chapter 14

1. https://simplepoll.rocks
2. https://bit.ly/nog-cram
3. https://bit.ly/nog-multi

Chapter 15

1. https://bit.ly/phil-wrike
2. https://bit.ly/slack-api
3. https://bit.ly/2GMTNGK

4. https://bit.ly/nog-zm-voice
5. https://bit.ly/zfd-inter
6. https://bit.ly/nog-mstog
7. https://bit.ly/nog-zoom-tog
8. https://bit.ly/nog-sconn
9. https://bit.ly/simon-nog1
10. https://bit.ly/owl-state

Chapter 16

1. https://bit.ly/hsc-wrike-simon
2. https://bit.ly/hsc-17hats

Made in the USA
Las Vegas, NV
27 September 2021